D0775129

FRONTIER PEOPLES OF CENTRAL NIGERIA

AND A STRATEGY FOR OUTREACH

A CATALOG OF SELECTED
DOVER BOOKS
IN ALL FIELDS OF INTEREST

A CATALOG OF SELECTED DOVER
BOOKS IN ALL FIELDS OF INTEREST

CONCERNING THE SPIRITUAL IN ART, Wassily Kandinsky. Pioneering work by father of abstract art. Thoughts on color theory, nature of art. Analysis of earlier masters. 12 illustrations. 80pp. of text. 5⅜ × 8½.   23411-8 Pa. $3.95

ANIMALS: 1,419 Copyright-Free Illustrations of Mammals, Birds, Fish, Insects, etc., Jim Harter (ed.). Clear wood engravings present, in extremely lifelike poses, over 1,000 species of animals. One of the most extensive pictorial sourcebooks of its kind. Captions. Index. 284pp. 9 × 12.   23766-4 Pa. $11.95

CELTIC ART: The Methods of Construction, George Bain. Simple geometric techniques for making Celtic interlacements, spirals, Kells-type initials, animals, humans, etc. Over 500 illustrations. 160pp. 9 × 12. (USO)   22923-8 Pa. $8.95

AN ATLAS OF ANATOMY FOR ARTISTS, Fritz Schider. Most thorough reference work on art anatomy in the world. Hundreds of illustrations, including selections from works by Vesalius, Leonardo, Goya, Ingres, Michelangelo, others. 593 illustrations. 192pp. 7⅛ × 10¼.   20241-0 Pa. $8.95

CELTIC HAND STROKE-BY-STROKE (Irish Half-Uncial from "The Book of Kells"): An Arthur Baker Calligraphy Manual, Arthur Baker. Complete guide to creating each letter of the alphabet in distinctive Celtic manner. Covers hand position, strokes, pens, inks, paper, more. Illustrated. 48pp. 8¼ × 11.
24336-2 Pa. $3.95

EASY ORIGAMI, John Montroll. Charming collection of 32 projects (hat, cup, pelican, piano, swan, many more) specially designed for the novice origami hobbyist. Clearly illustrated easy-to-follow instructions insure that even beginning papercrafters will achieve successful results. 48pp. 8¼ × 11.   27298-2 Pa. $2.95

THE COMPLETE BOOK OF BIRDHOUSE CONSTRUCTION FOR WOOD-WORKERS, Scott D. Campbell. Detailed instructions, illustrations, tables. Also data on bird habitat and instinct patterns. Bibliography. 3 tables. 63 illustrations in 15 figures. 48pp. 5¼ × 8½.   24407-5 Pa. $1.95

BLOOMINGDALE'S ILLUSTRATED 1886 CATALOG: Fashions, Dry Goods and Housewares, Bloomingdale Brothers. Famed merchants' extremely rare catalog depicting about 1,700 products: clothing, housewares, firearms, dry goods, jewelry, more. Invaluable for dating, identifying vintage items. Also, copyright-free graphics for artists, designers. Co-published with Henry Ford Museum & Greenfield Village. 160pp. 8¼ × 11.   25780-0 Pa. $9.95

HISTORIC COSTUME IN PICTURES, Braun & Schneider. Over 1,450 costumed figures in clearly detailed engravings—from dawn of civilization to end of 19th century. Captions. Many folk costumes. 256pp. 8⅜ × 11¾.   23150-X Pa. $10.95

STICKLEY CRAFTSMAN FURNITURE CATALOGS, Gustav Stickley and L. & J. G. Stickley. Beautiful, functional furniture in two authentic catalogs from 1910. 594 illustrations, including 277 photos, show settles, rockers, armchairs, reclining chairs, bookcases, desks, tables. 183pp. 6½ × 9¼. 23838-5 Pa. $8.95

AMERICAN LOCOMOTIVES IN HISTORIC PHOTOGRAPHS: 1858 to 1949, Ron Ziel (ed.). A rare collection of 126 meticulously detailed official photographs, called "builder portraits," of American locomotives that majestically chronicle the rise of steam locomotive power in America. Introduction. Detailed captions. xi + 129pp. 9 × 12. 27393-8 Pa. $12.95

AMERICA'S LIGHTHOUSES: An Illustrated History, Francis Ross Holland, Jr. Delightfully written, profusely illustrated fact-filled survey of over 200 American lighthouses since 1716. History, anecdotes, technological advances, more. 240pp. 8 × 10¾. 25576-X Pa. $11.95

TOWARDS A NEW ARCHITECTURE, Le Corbusier. Pioneering manifesto by founder of "International School." Technical and aesthetic theories, views of industry, economics, relation of form to function, "mass-production split" and much more. Profusely illustrated. 320pp. 6⅛ × 9¼. (USO) 25023-7 Pa. $8.95

HOW THE OTHER HALF LIVES, Jacob Riis. Famous journalistic record, exposing poverty and degradation of New York slums around 1900, by major social reformer. 100 striking and influential photographs. 233pp. 10 × 7⅞. 22012-5 Pa $10.95

FRUIT KEY AND TWIG KEY TO TREES AND SHRUBS, William M. Harlow. One of the handiest and most widely used identification aids. Fruit key covers 120 deciduous and evergreen species; twig key 160 deciduous species. Easily used. Over 300 photographs. 126pp. 5⅜ × 8½. 20511-8 Pa. $3.95

COMMON BIRD SONGS, Dr. Donald J. Borror. Songs of 60 most common U.S. birds: robins, sparrows, cardinals, bluejays, finches, more—arranged in order of increasing complexity. Up to 9 variations of songs of each species. Cassette and manual 99911-4 $8.95

ORCHIDS AS HOUSE PLANTS, Rebecca Tyson Northen. Grow cattleyas and many other kinds of orchids—in a window, in a case, or under artificial light. 63 illustrations. 148pp. 5⅜ × 8½. 23261-1 Pa. $3.95

MONSTER MAZES, Dave Phillips. Masterful mazes at four levels of difficulty. Avoid deadly perils and evil creatures to find magical treasures. Solutions for all 32 exciting illustrated puzzles. 48pp. 8¼ × 11. 26005-4 Pa. $2.95

MOZART'S DON GIOVANNI (DOVER OPERA LIBRETTO SERIES), Wolfgang Amadeus Mozart. Introduced and translated by Ellen H. Bleiler. Standard Italian libretto, with complete English translation. Convenient and thoroughly portable—an ideal companion for reading along with a recording or the performance itself. Introduction. List of characters. Plot summary. 121pp. 5¼ × 8½. 24944-1 Pa. $2.95

TECHNICAL MANUAL AND DICTIONARY OF CLASSICAL BALLET, Gail Grant. Defines, explains, comments on steps, movements, poses and concepts. 15-page pictorial section. Basic book for student, viewer. 127pp. 5⅜ × 8½. 21843-0 Pa. $3.95

BRASS INSTRUMENTS: Their History and Development, Anthony Baines. Authoritative, updated survey of the evolution of trumpets, trombones, bugles, cornets, French horns, tubas and other brass wind instruments. Over 140 illustrations and 48 music examples. Corrected and updated by author. New preface. Bibliography. 320pp. 5⅜ × 8½.   27574-4 Pa. $9.95

HOLLYWOOD GLAMOR PORTRAITS, John Kobal (ed.). 145 photos from 1926–49. Harlow, Gable, Bogart, Bacall; 94 stars in all. Full background on photographers, technical aspects. 160pp. 8⅜ × 11¼.   23352-9 Pa. $9.95

MAX AND MORITZ, Wilhelm Busch. Great humor classic in both German and English. Also 10 other works: "Cat and Mouse," "Plisch and Plumm," etc. 216pp. 5⅜ × 8½.   20181-3 Pa. $5.95

THE RAVEN AND OTHER FAVORITE POEMS, Edgar Allan Poe. Over 40 of the author's most memorable poems: "The Bells," "Ulalume," "Israfel," "To Helen," "The Conqueror Worm," "Eldorado," "Annabel Lee," many more. Alphabetic lists of titles and first lines. 64pp. 5³⁄₁₆ × 8¼.   26685-0 Pa. $1.00

SEVEN SCIENCE FICTION NOVELS, H. G. Wells. The standard collection of the great novels. Complete, unabridged. First Men in the Moon, Island of Dr. Moreau, War of the Worlds, Food of the Gods, Invisible Man, Time Machine, In the Days of the Comet. Total of 1,015pp. 5⅜ × 8½. (USO)   20264-X Clothbd. $29.95

AMULETS AND SUPERSTITIONS, E. A. Wallis Budge. Comprehensive discourse on origin, powers of amulets in many ancient cultures: Arab, Persian, Babylonian, Assyrian, Egyptian, Gnostic, Hebrew, Phoenician, Syriac, etc. Covers cross, swastika, crucifix, seals, rings, stones, etc. 584pp. 5⅜ × 8½. 23573-4 Pa. $12.95

RUSSIAN STORIES/PYCCKNE PACCKA3bl: A Dual-Language Book, edited by Gleb Struve. Twelve tales by such masters as Chekhov, Tolstoy, Dostoevsky, Pushkin, others. Excellent word-for-word English translations on facing pages, plus teaching and study aids, Russian/English vocabulary, biographical/critical introductions, more. 416pp. 5⅜ × 8½.   26244-8 Pa. $8.95

PHILADELPHIA THEN AND NOW: 60 Sites Photographed in the Past and Present, Kenneth Finkel and Susan Oyama. Rare photographs of City Hall, Logan Square, Independence Hall, Betsy Ross House, other landmarks juxtaposed with contemporary views. Captures changing face of historic city. Introduction. Captions. 128pp. 8¼ × 11.   25790-8 Pa. $9.95

AIA ARCHITECTURAL GUIDE TO NASSAU AND SUFFOLK COUNTIES, LONG ISLAND, The American Institute of Architects, Long Island Chapter, and the Society for the Preservation of Long Island Antiquities. Comprehensive, well-researched and generously illustrated volume brings to life over three centuries of Long Island's great architectural heritage. More than 240 photographs with authoritative, extensively detailed captions. 176pp. 8¼ × 11.   26946-9 Pa. $14.95

NORTH AMERICAN INDIAN LIFE: Customs and Traditions of 23 Tribes, Elsie Clews Parsons (ed.). 27 fictionalized essays by noted anthropologists examine religion, customs, government, additional facets of life among the Winnebago, Crow, Zuni, Eskimo, other tribes. 480pp. 6⅛ × 9¼.   27377-6 Pa. $10.95

FRANK LLOYD WRIGHT'S HOLLYHOCK HOUSE, Donald Hoffmann. Lavishly illustrated, carefully documented study of one of Wright's most controversial residential designs. Over 120 photographs, floor plans, elevations, etc. Detailed perceptive text by noted Wright scholar. Index. 128pp. 9¼ × 10¾.
27133-1 Pa. $11.95

THE MALE AND FEMALE FIGURE IN MOTION: 60 Classic Photographic Sequences, Eadweard Muybridge. 60 true action photographs of men and women walking, running, climbing, bending, turning, etc., reproduced from rare 19th-century masterpiece. vi + 121pp. 9 × 12. 24745-7 Pa. $10.95

1001 QUESTIONS ANSWERED ABOUT THE SEASHORE, N. J. Berrill and Jacquelyn Berrill. Queries answered about dolphins, sea snails, sponges, starfish, fishes, shore birds, many others. Covers appearance, breeding, growth, feeding, much more. 305pp. 5¼ × 8¼. 23366-9 Pa. $7.95

GUIDE TO OWL WATCHING IN NORTH AMERICA, Donald S. Heintzelman. Superb guide offers complete data and descriptions of 19 species: barn owl, screech owl, snowy owl, many more. Expert coverage of owl-watching equipment, conservation, migrations and invasions, etc. Guide to observing sites. 84 illustrations. xiii + 193pp. 5⅜ × 8½. 27344-X Pa. $7.95

MEDICINAL AND OTHER USES OF NORTH AMERICAN PLANTS: A Historical Survey with Special Reference to the Eastern Indian Tribes, Charlotte Erichsen-Brown. Chronological historical citations document 500 years of usage of plants, trees, shrubs native to eastern Canada, northeastern U.S. Also complete identifying information. 343 illustrations. 544pp. 6½ × 9¼. 25951-X Pa. $12.95

STORYBOOK MAZES, Dave Phillips. 23 stories and mazes on two-page spreads: Wizard of Oz, Treasure Island, Robin Hood, etc. Solutions. 64pp. 8¼ × 11.
23628-5 Pa. $2.95

NEGRO FOLK MUSIC, U.S.A., Harold Courlander. Noted folklorist's scholarly yet readable analysis of rich and varied musical tradition. Includes authentic versions of over 40 folk songs. Valuable bibliography and discography. xi + 324pp. 5⅜ × 8½. 27350-4 Pa. $7.95

MOVIE-STAR PORTRAITS OF THE FORTIES, John Kobal (ed.). 163 glamor, studio photos of 106 stars of the 1940s: Rita Hayworth, Ava Gardner, Marlon Brando, Clark Gable, many more. 176pp. 8⅜ × 11¼. 23546-7 Pa. $10.95

BENCHLEY LOST AND FOUND, Robert Benchley. Finest humor from early 30s, about pet peeves, child psychologists, post office and others. Mostly unavailable elsewhere. 73 illustrations by Peter Arno and others. 183pp. 5⅜ × 8½.
22410-4 Pa. $5.95

YEKL and THE IMPORTED BRIDEGROOM AND OTHER STORIES OF YIDDISH NEW YORK, Abraham Cahan. Film Hester Street based on Yekl (1896). Novel, other stories among first about Jewish immigrants on N.Y.'s East Side. 240pp. 5⅜ × 8½. 22427-9 Pa. $5.95

SELECTED POEMS, Walt Whitman. Generous sampling from *Leaves of Grass.* Twenty-four poems include "I Hear America Singing," "Song of the Open Road," "I Sing the Body Electric," "When Lilacs Last in the Dooryard Bloom'd," "O Captain! My Captain!"—all reprinted from an authoritative edition. Lists of titles and first lines. 128pp. 5³⁄₁₆ × 8¼. 26878-0 Pa. $1.00

THE BEST TALES OF HOFFMANN, E. T. A. Hoffmann. 10 of Hoffmann's most important stories: "Nutcracker and the King of Mice," "The Golden Flowerpot," etc. 458pp. 5⅜ × 8½.   21793-0 Pa. $8.95

FROM FETISH TO GOD IN ANCIENT EGYPT, E. A. Wallis Budge. Rich detailed survey of Egyptian conception of "God" and gods, magic, cult of animals, Osiris, more. Also, superb English translations of hymns and legends. 240 illustrations. 545pp. 5⅜ × 8½.   25803-3 Pa. $11.95

FRENCH STORIES/CONTES FRANÇAIS: A Dual-Language Book, Wallace Fowlie. Ten stories by French masters, Voltaire to Camus: "Micromegas" by Voltaire; "The Atheist's Mass" by Balzac; "Minuet" by de Maupassant; "The Guest" by Camus, six more. Excellent English translations on facing pages. Also French-English vocabulary list, exercises, more. 352pp. 5⅜ × 8½. 26443-2 Pa. $8.95

CHICAGO AT THE TURN OF THE CENTURY IN PHOTOGRAPHS: 122 Historic Views from the Collections of the Chicago Historical Society, Larry A. Viskochil. Rare large-format prints offer detailed views of City Hall, State Street, the Loop, Hull House, Union Station, many other landmarks, circa 1904-1913. Introduction. Captions. Maps. 144pp. 9⅜ × 12¼.   24656-6 Pa. $12.95

OLD BROOKLYN IN EARLY PHOTOGRAPHS, 1865-1929, William Lee Younger. Luna Park, Gravesend race track, construction of Grand Army Plaza, moving of Hotel Brighton, etc. 157 previously unpublished photographs. 165pp. 8⅞ × 11¾.   23587-4 Pa. $12.95

THE MYTHS OF THE NORTH AMERICAN INDIANS, Lewis Spence. Rich anthology of the myths and legends of the Algonquins, Iroquois, Pawnees and Sioux, prefaced by an extensive historical and ethnological commentary. 36 illustrations. 480pp. 5⅜ × 8½.   25967-6 Pa. $8.95

AN ENCYCLOPEDIA OF BATTLES: Accounts of Over 1,560 Battles from 1479 B.C. to the Present, David Eggenberger. Essential details of every major battle in recorded history from the first battle of Megiddo in 1479 B.C. to Grenada in 1984. List of Battle Maps. New Appendix covering the years 1967-1984. Index. 99 illustrations. 544pp. 6½ × 9¼.   24913-1 Pa. $14.95

SAILING ALONE AROUND THE WORLD, Captain Joshua Slocum. First man to sail around the world, alone, in small boat. One of great feats of seamanship told in delightful manner. 67 illustrations. 294pp. 5⅜ × 8½.   20326-3 Pa. $5.95

ANARCHISM AND OTHER ESSAYS, Emma Goldman. Powerful, penetrating, prophetic essays on direct action, role of minorities, prison reform, puritan hypocrisy, violence, etc. 271pp. 5⅜ × 8½.   22484-8 Pa. $5.95

MYTHS OF THE HINDUS AND BUDDHISTS, Ananda K. Coomaraswamy and Sister Nivedita. Great stories of the epics; deeds of Krishna, Shiva, taken from puranas, Vedas, folk tales; etc. 32 illustrations. 400pp. 5⅜ × 8½. 21759-0 Pa. $9.95

BEYOND PSYCHOLOGY, Otto Rank. Fear of death, desire of immortality, nature of sexuality, social organization, creativity, according to Rankian system. 291pp. 5⅜ × 8½.   20485-5 Pa. $7.95

A THEOLOGICO-POLITICAL TREATISE, Benedict Spinoza. Also contains unfinished Political Treatise. Great classic on religious liberty, theory of government on common consent. R. Elwes translation. Total of 421pp. 5⅜ × 8½.
                                                                        20249-6 Pa. $7.95

MY BONDAGE AND MY FREEDOM, Frederick Douglass. Born a slave, Douglass became outspoken force in antislavery movement. The best of Douglass' autobiographies. Graphic description of slave life. 464pp. 5⅜ × 8½. 22457-0 Pa. $8.95

FOLLOWING THE EQUATOR: A Journey Around the World, Mark Twain. Fascinating humorous account of 1897 voyage to Hawaii, Australia, India, New Zealand, etc. Ironic, bemused reports on peoples, customs, climate, flora and fauna, politics, much more. 197 illustrations. 720pp. 5⅜ × 8½. 26113-1 Pa. $15.95

THE PEOPLE CALLED SHAKERS, Edward D. Andrews. Definitive study of Shakers: origins, beliefs, practices, dances, social organization, furniture and crafts, etc. 33 illustrations. 351pp. 5⅜ × 8½. 21081-2 Pa. $7.95

THE MYTHS OF GREECE AND ROME, H. A. Guerber. A classic of mythology, generously illustrated, long prized for its simple, graphic, accurate retelling of the principal myths of Greece and Rome, and for its commentary on their origins and significance. With 64 illustrations by Michelangelo, Raphael, Titian, Rubens, Canova, Bernini and others. 480pp. 5⅜ × 8½. 27584-1 Pa. $9.95

PSYCHOLOGY OF MUSIC, Carl E. Seashore. Classic work discusses music as a medium from psychological viewpoint. Clear treatment of physical acoustics, auditory apparatus, sound perception, development of musical skills, nature of musical feeling, host of other topics. 88 figures. 408pp. 5⅜ × 8½. 21851-1 Pa. $9.95

THE PHILOSOPHY OF HISTORY, Georg W. Hegel. Great classic of Western thought develops concept that history is not chance but rational process, the evolution of freedom. 457pp. 5⅜ × 8½. 20112-0 Pa. $8.95

THE BOOK OF TEA, Kakuzo Okakura. Minor classic of the Orient: entertaining, charming explanation, interpretation of traditional Japanese culture in terms of tea ceremony. 94pp. 5⅜ × 8½. 20070-1 Pa. $2.95

LIFE IN ANCIENT EGYPT, Adolf Erman. Fullest, most thorough, detailed older account with much not in more recent books, domestic life, religion, magic, medicine, commerce, much more. Many illustrations reproduce tomb paintings, carvings, hieroglyphs, etc. 597pp. 5⅜ × 8½. 22632-8 Pa. $9.95

SUNDIALS, Their Theory and Construction, Albert Waugh. Far and away the best, most thorough coverage of ideas, mathematics concerned, types, construction, adjusting anywhere. Simple, nontechnical treatment allows even children to build several of these dials. Over 100 illustrations. 230pp. 5⅜ × 8½. 22947-5 Pa. $5.95

DYNAMICS OF FLUIDS IN POROUS MEDIA, Jacob Bear. For advanced students of ground water hydrology, soil mechanics and physics, drainage and irrigation engineering, and more. 335 illustrations. Exercises, with answers. 784pp. 6⅛ × 9¼. 65675-6 Pa. $19.95

SONGS OF EXPERIENCE: Facsimile Reproduction with 26 Plates in Full Color, William Blake. 26 full-color plates from a rare 1826 edition. Includes "The Tyger," "London," "Holy Thursday," and other poems. Printed text of poems. 48pp. 5¼ × 7. 24636-1 Pa. $3.95

OLD-TIME VIGNETTES IN FULL COLOR, Carol Belanger Grafton (ed.). Over 390 charming, often sentimental illustrations, selected from archives of Victorian graphics—pretty women posing, children playing, food, flowers, kittens and puppies, smiling cherubs, birds and butterflies, much more. All copyright-free. 48pp. 9¼ × 12¼. 27269-9 Pa. $5.95

PERSPECTIVE FOR ARTISTS, Rex Vicat Cole. Depth, perspective of sky and sea, shadows, much more, not usually covered. 391 diagrams, 81 reproductions of drawings and paintings. 279pp. 5⅜ × 8½. 22487-2 Pa. $6.95

DRAWING THE LIVING FIGURE, Joseph Sheppard. Innovative approach to artistic anatomy focuses on specifics of surface anatomy, rather than muscles and bones. Over 170 drawings of live models in front, back and side views, and in widely varying poses. Accompanying diagrams. 177 illustrations. Introduction. Index. 144pp. 8⅜ × 11¼. 26723-7 Pa. $7.95

GOTHIC AND OLD ENGLISH ALPHABETS: 100 Complete Fonts, Dan X. Solo. Add power, elegance to posters, signs, other graphics with 100 stunning copyright-free alphabets: Blackstone, Dolbey, Germania, 97 more—including many lower-case, numerals, punctuation marks. 104pp. 8⅛ × 11. 24695-7 Pa. $7.95

HOW TO DO BEADWORK, Mary White. Fundamental book on craft from simple projects to five-bead chains and woven works. 106 illustrations. 142pp. 5⅜ × 8. 20697-1 Pa. $4.95

THE BOOK OF WOOD CARVING, Charles Marshall Sayers. Finest book for beginners discusses fundamentals and offers 34 designs. "Absolutely first rate . . . well thought out and well executed."—E. J. Tangerman. 118pp. 7¾ × 10⅝. 23654-4 Pa. $5.95

ILLUSTRATED CATALOG OF CIVIL WAR MILITARY GOODS: Union Army Weapons, Insignia, Uniform Accessories, and Other Equipment, Schuyler, Hartley, and Graham. Rare, profusely illustrated 1846 catalog includes Union Army uniform and dress regulations, arms and ammunition, coats, insignia, flags, swords, rifles, etc. 226 illustrations. 160pp. 9 × 12. 24939-5 Pa. $10.95

WOMEN'S FASHIONS OF THE EARLY 1900s: An Unabridged Republication of "New York Fashions, 1909," National Cloak & Suit Co. Rare catalog of mail-order fashions documents women's and children's clothing styles shortly after the turn of the century. Captions offer full descriptions, prices. Invaluable resource for fashion, costume historians. Approximately 725 illustrations. 128pp. 8⅜ × 11¼. 27276-1 Pa. $10.95

THE 1912 AND 1915 GUSTAV STICKLEY FURNITURE CATALOGS, Gustav Stickley. With over 200 detailed illustrations and descriptions, these two catalogs are essential reading and reference materials and identification guides for Stickley furniture. Captions cite materials, dimensions and prices. 112pp. 6½ × 9¼. 26676-1 Pa. $9.95

EARLY AMERICAN LOCOMOTIVES, John H. White, Jr. Finest locomotive engravings from early 19th century: historical (1804–74), main-line (after 1870), special, foreign, etc. 147 plates. 142pp. 11⅜ × 8¼. 22772-3 Pa. $8.95

THE TALL SHIPS OF TODAY IN PHOTOGRAPHS, Frank O. Braynard. Lavishly illustrated tribute to nearly 100 majestic contemporary sailing vessels: Amerigo Vespucci, Clearwater, Constitution, Eagle, Mayflower, Sea Cloud, Victory, many more. Authoritative captions provide statistics, background on each ship. 190 black-and-white photographs and illustrations. Introduction. 128pp. 8⅞ × 11¾. 27163-3 Pa. $12.95

EARLY NINETEENTH-CENTURY CRAFTS AND TRADES, Peter Stockham (ed.). Extremely rare 1807 volume describes to youngsters the crafts and trades of the day: brickmaker, weaver, dressmaker, bookbinder, ropemaker, saddler, many more. Quaint prose, charming illustrations for each craft. 20 black-and-white line illustrations. 192pp. 4⅝ × 6. 27293-1 Pa. $4.95

VICTORIAN FASHIONS AND COSTUMES FROM HARPER'S BAZAR, 1867–1898, Stella Blum (ed.). Day costumes, evening wear, sports clothes, shoes, hats, other accessories in over 1,000 detailed engravings. 320pp. 9⅜ × 12¼. 22990-4 Pa. $13.95

GUSTAV STICKLEY, THE CRAFTSMAN, Mary Ann Smith. Superb study surveys broad scope of Stickley's achievement, especially in architecture. Design philosophy, rise and fall of the Craftsman empire, descriptions and floor plans for many Craftsman houses, more. 86 black-and-white halftones. 31 line illustrations. Introduction. 208pp. 6½ × 9¼. 27210-9 Pa. $9.95

THE LONG ISLAND RAIL ROAD IN EARLY PHOTOGRAPHS, Ron Ziel. Over 220 rare photos, informative text document origin (1844) and development of rail service on Long Island. Vintage views of early trains, locomotives, stations, passengers, crews, much more. Captions. 8⅞ × 11¾. 26301-0 Pa. $13.95

THE BOOK OF OLD SHIPS: From Egyptian Galleys to Clipper Ships, Henry B. Culver. Superb, authoritative history of sailing vessels, with 80 magnificent line illustrations. Galley, bark, caravel, longship, whaler, many more. Detailed, informative text on each vessel by noted naval historian. Introduction. 256pp. 5⅜ × 8½. 27332-6 Pa. $6.95

TEN BOOKS ON ARCHITECTURE, Vitruvius. The most important book ever written on architecture. Early Roman aesthetics, technology, classical orders, site selection, all other aspects. Morgan translation. 331pp. 5⅜ × 8½. 20645-9 Pa. $8.95

THE HUMAN FIGURE IN MOTION, Eadweard Muybridge. More than 4,500 stopped-action photos, in action series, showing undraped men, women, children jumping, lying down, throwing, sitting, wrestling, carrying, etc. 390pp. 7⅞ × 10⅝. 20204-6 Clothbd. $24.95

TREES OF THE EASTERN AND CENTRAL UNITED STATES AND CANADA, William M. Harlow. Best one-volume guide to 140 trees. Full descriptions, woodlore, range, etc. Over 600 illustrations. Handy size. 288pp. 4½ × 6⅜. 20395-6 Pa. $5.95

SONGS OF WESTERN BIRDS, Dr. Donald J. Borror. Complete song and call repertoire of 60 western species, including flycatchers, juncoes, cactus wrens, many more—includes fully illustrated booklet. Cassette and manual 99913-0 $8.95

GROWING AND USING HERBS AND SPICES, Milo Miloradovich. Versatile handbook provides all the information needed for cultivation and use of all the herbs and spices available in North America. 4 illustrations. Index. Glossary. 236pp. 5⅜ × 8½. 25058-X Pa. $5.95

BIG BOOK OF MAZES AND LABYRINTHS, Walter Shepherd. 50 mazes and labyrinths in all—classical, solid, ripple, and more—in one great volume. Perfect inexpensive puzzler for clever youngsters. Full solutions. 112pp. 8⅛ × 11. 22951-3 Pa. $3.95

PIANO TUNING, J. Cree Fischer. Clearest, best book for beginner, amateur. Simple repairs, raising dropped notes, tuning by easy method of flattened fifths. No previous skills needed. 4 illustrations. 201pp. 5⅜ × 8½. 23267-0 Pa. $5.95

A SOURCE BOOK IN THEATRICAL HISTORY, A. M. Nagler. Contemporary observers on acting, directing, make-up, costuming, stage props, machinery, scene design, from Ancient Greece to Chekhov. 611pp. 5⅜ × 8½. 20515-0 Pa. $11.95

THE COMPLETE NONSENSE OF EDWARD LEAR, Edward Lear. All nonsense limericks, zany alphabets, Owl and Pussycat, songs, nonsense botany, etc., illustrated by Lear. Total of 320pp. 5⅜ × 8½. (USO) 20167-8 Pa. $5.95

VICTORIAN PARLOUR POETRY: An Annotated Anthology, Michael R. Turner. 117 gems by Longfellow, Tennyson, Browning, many lesser-known poets. "The Village Blacksmith," "Curfew Must Not Ring Tonight," "Only a Baby Small," dozens more, often difficult to find elsewhere. Index of poets, titles, first lines. xxiii + 325pp. 5⅜ × 8¼. 27044-0 Pa. $8.95

DUBLINERS, James Joyce. Fifteen stories offer vivid, tightly focused observations of the lives of Dublin's poorer classes. At least one, "The Dead," is considered a masterpiece. Reprinted complete and unabridged from standard edition. 160pp. 5³⁄₁₆ × 8¼. 26870-5 Pa. $1.00

THE HAUNTED MONASTERY and THE CHINESE MAZE MURDERS, Robert van Gulik. Two full novels by van Gulik, set in 7th-century China, continue adventures of Judge Dee and his companions. An evil Taoist monastery, seemingly supernatural events; overgrown topiary maze hides strange crimes. 27 illustrations. 328pp. 5⅜ × 8½. 23502-5 Pa. $7.95

THE BOOK OF THE SACRED MAGIC OF ABRAMELIN THE MAGE, translated by S. MacGregor Mathers. Medieval manuscript of ceremonial magic. Basic document in Aleister Crowley, Golden Dawn groups. 268pp. 5⅜ × 8½. 23211-5 Pa. $7.95

NEW RUSSIAN-ENGLISH AND ENGLISH-RUSSIAN DICTIONARY, M. A. O'Brien. This is a remarkably handy Russian dictionary, containing a surprising amount of information, including over 70,000 entries. 366pp. 4½ × 6⅛. 20208-9 Pa. $8.95

HISTORIC HOMES OF THE AMERICAN PRESIDENTS, Second, Revised Edition, Irvin Haas. A traveler's guide to American Presidential homes, most open to the public, depicting and describing homes occupied by every American President from George Washington to George Bush. With visiting hours, admission charges, travel routes. 175 photographs. Index. 160pp. 8¼ × 11. 26751-2 Pa. $10.95

NEW YORK IN THE FORTIES, Andreas Feininger. 162 brilliant photographs by the well-known photographer, formerly with *Life* magazine. Commuters, shoppers, Times Square at night, much else from city at its peak. Captions by John von Hartz. 181pp. 9¼ × 10¾. 23585-8 Pa. $12.95

INDIAN SIGN LANGUAGE, William Tomkins. Over 525 signs developed by Sioux and other tribes. Written instructions and diagrams. Also 290 pictographs. 111pp. 6⅛ × 9¼. 22029-X Pa. $3.50

CATALOG OF DOVER BOOKS

THE INFLUENCE OF SEA POWER UPON HISTORY, 1660–1783, A. T. Mahan. Influential classic of naval history and tactics still used as text in war colleges. First paperback edition. 4 maps. 24 battle plans. 640pp. 5⅜ × 8½.
25509-3 Pa. $12.95

THE STORY OF THE TITANIC AS TOLD BY ITS SURVIVORS, Jack Winocour (ed.). What it was really like. Panic, despair, shocking inefficiency, and a little heroism. More thrilling than any fictional account. 26 illustrations. 320pp. 5⅜ × 8½.
20610-6 Pa. $7.95

FAIRY AND FOLK TALES OF THE IRISH PEASANTRY, William Butler Yeats (ed.). Treasury of 64 tales from the twilight world of Celtic myth and legend: "The Soul Cages," "The Kildare Pooka," "King O'Toole and his Goose," many more. Introduction and Notes by W. B. Yeats. 352pp. 5⅜ × 8½.
26941-8 Pa. $7.95

BUDDHIST MAHAYANA TEXTS, E. B. Cowell and Others (eds.). Superb, accurate translations of basic documents in Mahayana Buddhism, highly important in history of religions. The Buddha-karita of Asvaghosha, Larger Sukhavativyuha, more. 448pp. 5⅜ × 8½. ,
25552-2 Pa. $9.95

ONE TWO THREE . . . INFINITY: Facts and Speculations of Science, George Gamow. Great physicist's fascinating, readable overview of contemporary science: number theory, relativity, fourth dimension, entropy, genes, atomic structure, much more. 128 illustrations. Index. 352pp. 5⅜ × 8½.
25664-2 Pa. $8.95

ENGINEERING IN HISTORY, Richard Shelton Kirby, et al. Broad, nontechnical survey of history's major technological advances: birth of Greek science, industrial revolution, electricity and applied science, 20th-century automation, much more. 181 illustrations. ". . . excellent . . ."—Isis. Bibliography. vii + 530pp. 5⅜ × 8¼.
26412-2 Pa. $14.95

Prices subject to change without notice.
Available at your book dealer or write for free catalog to Dept. GI, Dover Publications, Inc., 31 East 2nd St., Mineola, N.Y. 11501. Dover publishes more than 500 books each year on science, elementary and advanced mathematics, biology, music, art, literary history, social sciences and other areas.

BV
3777
N54
S913

FRONTIER
PEOPLES
OF CENTRAL NIGERIA
and a strategy for outreach.

gerald o. swank

William Carey Library

533 HERMOSA STREET • SOUTH PASADENA, CALIF. 91030

13381

WITHDRAWN
PACIFIC COLLEGE - M. B. SEMINARY
FRESNO, CALIF. 93702

Copyright © 1977 by the William Carey Library

All rights reserved.

No part of this book may be used or reproduced in any manner
whatsoever without written permission, except in the case of brief
quotations embodied in critical articles and reviews.

Library of Congress Catalog Card Number 77-9944
International Standard Book Number 0-87808-154-2

In accord with some of the most recent thinking in the aca-
demic press, the William Carey Library is pleased to present
this scholarly book which has been prepared from an author-
edited and author-prepared camera-ready manuscript.

Order additional copies from:

Nigeria Evangelical		William Carey Library
Fellowship	or	1705 N. Sierra Bonita
Ilorin, Kwara State		Pasadena, California
Nigeria		U.S.A.

Published by the William Carey Library
533 Hermosa Street
South Pasadena, Calif. 91030
Telephone 213-682-2047

PRINTED IN THE UNITED STATES OF AMERICA

Contents

PART I

THE TARGET GROUPS

v

PART II

COMMENTS ON CULTURE

PART III

STRATEGY: STEPS FOR EVANGELISM AND CHURCH PLANTING

APPENDICES

Tables

Acknowledgments

To Sudan Interior Mission, and particularly Mr. Trevor Ardill, U.S.A. Director, for giving me the time and liberty for the research, writing and translation involved in this project.

To Nigeria Evangelical Fellowship for their enthusiasm and vision for this project together with generous provision of funds to enable it to be carried out.

To Mr. Mohammed Abdul, a brilliant and dedicated Nigerian studying at the University of Nebraska, who is very facile in both English and Hausa languages, for valuable assistance in the translation of this book into the Hausa language.

To Dorothy, my devoted wife, whose constant encouragement and understanding have been a source of inspiration to me, and also for her patience during long periods of separation while I was in Africa.

To Vera Crouch, S.I.M. co-worker, who did such an excellent piece of work in typing both the Hausa and English manuscripts.

To all those, both Nigerians and expatriates, who gave much time to the answering of questions and participation in discussions, thus making the facts of this book available.

Foreword

(To the *Report on Frontier Situations in Central Nigeria and Suggested Strategy for Evangelism and Church Planting.*)

Anyone who knows anything about "big game hunting" in Africa, knows well that one doesn't just set out into the bush with gun in hand and with little or no previous knowledge or experience. The more the hunter knows about the size, nature and number of the animals that roam the bush -- about their distinctive characteristics and habits -- the more successful he will be in "the kill." On the basis of this information, he also is aware of how crucial it is to use the right strategy -- weapons, ammunition and approach -- and how necessary it is to take careful aim. He never shoots blindly or prematurely into the brush.

Evangelism is "big game hunting." To be successful it requires careful research -- an intimate knowledge of target groups, of their distinctive religious and cultural characteristics, the degree to which the gospel has penetrated, and a strategy that will effectively win whole families and tribes to Jesus Christ.

In this incisive report Gerald Swank and his team of Nigerian researchers have given us just that in regard to 30 ethnic groups of Central Nigeria. The Study has been made at the request of the Nigerian Evangelical Fellowship. It pinpoints the extent to which each target group has or has not been evangelized and their readiness for change. It zeros in on the cultural bridges that affect the communication of the gospel. And it puts this information into a form that the Nigerian Church can use in the completion of her God-commissioned evangelistic task.

ix

Every Christian in Nigeria should carefully and prayerfully read this report. It should be thoroughly studied by each denomination and local church. Its value lies not in its documentary details, nor its unique insights into the distinctive cultural patterns of each ethnic group. Its real value will be determined by what Nigerian evangelical Christians do with it now that God has placed it in their hands.

May God grant that as a result, the next ten years, should Jesus Christ tarry His coming, will see the greatest evangelistic upsurge the churches of Nigeria have ever experienced. And this Study is the first step!

Dr. Vergil Gerber
Executive Secretary
Evangelical Missions
Information Service

Preface

The Nigeria Evangelical Fellowship commissioned a survey of the unreached tribal groups of Central Nigeria. Questionnaires were mailed out in March 1975 to informed people including mission and church executives, pastors, teachers and missionaries. The questionnaire used for the Unreached Peoples File compiled for the International Congress on Evangelization, Lausanne, was modified to better meet the needs of the Nigerian situation. Forty-five tribes were selected as possibilities on the basis of the Unreached Peoples File, the list compiled by Dr. David Barrett and published in *The Gospel and Frontier Peoples*, editor R. Pierce Beaver, and personal knowledge and experience. During June, July and August interviews were conducted with knowledgeable representatives of these groups in 25 locations. Rev. Gerald Swank was the anchor man of the team and he was assisted by Pastor Sankwai Zamani, Principal of the ECWA Pastors Training School, Zabolo, Rev. Jacob Bawa, Principal UMCA Theological Seminary, Ilorin and Rev. Yakubu Yako, ECWA evangelist at large, Kaduna.

The report describes more than thirty unevangelized groups and those that have remained especially resistant to the gospel. No attempt is made to go into detail as this would have been impossible given the terms of reference of the study.

The purpose has been to present the kind of information that will enable the churches to understand the needs of these peoples and to lay the foundation for a strategy to complete their evangelization, thus encouraging church leaders to grapple with this task.

We can thank God that very likely every tribal group in the
Central Belt has at some time been exposed to the gospel message.
For some it has only been in passing. For others it has been many
years since the last messenger spoke to them and no church was
established. In many of those described the church has been planted
and is beginning to grow, albeit slowly.

It is regretted that statistics are less than accurate and incom-
plete. The Nigerian Census of 1973 was officially laid to rest while
this survey was in progress. It would have provided a great deal
of valuable data regarding the size of the tribal groups and their
religious preferences. Perhaps this will be available in the near
future. However in the area of church statistics there was also
a woeful lack of detail. We must know the size of the task before
us, the present socio-economic status of the people, and the potential
resources available to us. May this report stimulate a desire among
us all to gather such information.

Mention has already been made of the Unreached Peoples File and
The Gospel and Frontier Peoples. I am deeply indebted to these works
both for the materials in them and the motivation they initially
provided to undertake this survey. Another very valuable contribution was made by Dr. Edward Pentecost's book, *Reaching the Unreached*.
Everyone interested in this subject should obtain and read all three
of these books.

The description in *Frontier Peoples* (Barrett) does not include
those tribes that have been Islamized, that is, where more than 75%
of the members are professing Muslims. Likewise this report omits
these groups. They represent an entirely different situation and
it did not seem wise to put the two together. Some notable dif-
ferences will be found in the groups listed in this report when
compared with similar lists made during the past ten years. This
is due largely to the intensive evangelism efforts that are being
carried out in many areas as well as the fact that this survey was
conducted at the grassroots level and some former misconceptions
have been corrected.

This is only the beginning. I am well aware of the limitations
of this report. Everyone of you who is deeply concerned for these
peoples is urged to continue this kind of investigation. Any
additional information and corrections will be gladly received.

Definitions

Any attempt to describe the difference between evangelized
and the unevangelized is partially subjective and must be understood to be based largely on observers' estimates as well as on
available church growth figures.   Often the church statistics
are not given by groups but rather by districts which may include
several groups.   Another factor which has been an obstacle to
accuracy is the lack of a recent census.   The last published
one is 1964.

In his book *Reaching the Unreached*, Edward Pentecost quotes
the definition of unreached/unevangelized people that was accepted
by the Lausanne International Congress on World Evangelization.
(They are) "those homogenous units which have not received or
responded to the gospel. This unresponsiveness may be due to lack
of opportunity, lack of understanding, or because they have not
received sufficient information about the gospel message within
their own language, cultural frame of reference and communication
channels to make Christianity a viable option.

"...We consider that a people is unreached/unevangelized when
less than 20% are professing Christians. This assumes that a
people has a minority group attitude until that people reaches
15 to 20% of the population. At that point it may move into a
recognition of its own self-identity." (Pentecost, 1974:31).

To this Barrett substantially agrees. (Barrett, 1968:137).
But he goes beyond numerical evangelization and discusses cultural evangelization. "(It) goes beyond them as individuals or

groups to encompass also the penetration of their tribal philosophy and world-view by the Christian ethic and world-view. It is
for this reason that the translation of the Scriptures into a
tribe's own vernacular language is of such importance." (Barrett,
1973 in *The Gospel and Frontier Situations*).

The definitions given here are purposely simple but sufficient
to separate the categories on a pragmatic basis.

1. Evangelized or Reached people. A group in which 15-20%
   are professing Christians. Or 10% are Christians and there
is a strong progressive church able to complete the task throughout the group.

2. Unevangelized or Unreached people. A group in which 0-25%
   have heard the gospel and understood and only a few have
become Christian, usually less than 1%.

3. Partially evangelized. When 25-50% of a group have understood the gospel and a church has been established among
them.

4. Resistant. A group which is 50-100% evangelized, i.e. nearly
   all have had an adequate opportunity but less than 10% are
Christian.

5. Islamized. A group which is 75% or more Muslim and few
   believers.

In this report we are concerned with the people who come under
categories 2,3 & 4 above.

Abbreviations

INITIALS	NAME	ADDRESS
AC	Anglican Church, Box 72 Kaduna, Kaduna	
AG	Assemblies of God, Box 130 Jos, Plateau	
BAP	Baptist Convention of Nigeria, P.O. Box 118 Kaduna, Kaduna	
BM	Basel Mission, Gava via Gwoza via Maiduguri, Borno	
BSN	Bible Society of Nigeria, Box 2838, Lagos	
CAC	Christ Apostolic Church, Box 530 Ibadan, Oyo	
CCN	Christian Council of Nigeria, Box 2383, Lagos	
CBM	Church Brethren Mission, Box 676 Jos, Plateau	
CMML	Christian Missions Many Lands, Ayangba via Idah, Kwara	
CMS	Church Missionary Society, Wusasa Zaria, Kaduna	
ECWA	Evangelical Churches of West Africa, Box 63 Jos, Plateau	
EKAN	Church of Christ of Nigeria Plateau, Box 463 Jos, Plateau	
EKAS	BENUE, Box 38 Wukari, Benue (Church of Christ of Sudan)	
EKAS	EASTERN DISTRICT, Mubi, Gongola (Church of Christ of Sudan)	
EKAS	MADA HILLS, Alushi, Plateau (Church of Christ of Sudan)	
EKAS	UNITED METHODIST, Box 21 Jalingo via Yola, Gongola (Church of Christ of Sudan)	
EMS	Evangelical Missionary Society, Box 63 Jos, Plateau	
LCCS	Lutheran Church of Christ, Numan, Gongola	
NEF	Nigeria Evangelical Fellowship, PMB 1441 Ilorin, Kwara	
NLFA	New Life for All, P.O. Box 77 Jos, Plateau	
PRO	PROTESTANT	
QIM	QUA IBOE Mission, Box 4 Idah, Kwara	
RC	ROMAN CATHOLIC	
SIM	Sudan Interior Mission, Jos, Plateau	
SUM	Sudan United Mission, Box 463 Jos, Plateau	
SUM/BB	--British Branch, Box 463 Jos, Plateau	
SUM/CRC	--Christian Reformed Church, Box 261 Jos, Plateau	
SUM/Luth	--Danish Lutheran, Numan, Gongola	
SUM/MH	--Mada Hills, Alushi, Plateau	
SUM/UM	--United Methodist, c/o Dean Gilliland TCNN Bukuru, Plateau	
SIL	Summer Institute Linguistics (Wyclif Bible Translators) Jos	
UMCA	United Missionary Church Africa, Box 172 Ilorin, Kwara	
UMS	United Mission of Sudan, Box 172 Ilorin, Kwara	
UPE	Universal Primary Education	
XN	Christian	

PART I

THE TARGET GROUPS

PART I

THE TARGET
GROUPS

INTRODUCTION TO PART I

EXPLANATION: Please refer to the Data sheets at the close of this
report for specific information on each ethnic group
(Appendix A). *

In this section an effort is made to identify the following:

a) special features and distinctives of traditional religious
   worship
b) Nature of penetration of the gospel
c) major hindrances and encouragements to the progress of the
   gospel
d) resources available for further extension and expansion

A strategy plan is then suggested. This is based upon the
available data and the known cultural characteristics and the
potential resources. It must be emphasized that it is meant to be
a basic strategy set, and should be accepted in that way. Although
it may not have been tested in this particular situation, yet the
various components have been found useful in a variety of situations
and usually very effective. It is therefore reasonable to believe
that given the opportunity the combination of components set forth
here will be found effective in the proclamation of the gospel and
the planting of Christ's church among these target groups until more
light is thrown upon each situation. Without doubt there will occur
additions and modifications to this basic strategy set which will
further enhance its usefulness. In other words, here is a point
from which work can be planned and carried out. See section V on
Steps for Evangelism and Church Planting.

Why tribal groupings? Where deemed necessary attention is paid
to each ethnic group. Since our main purpose in this study is to
provide a suitable strategy for reaching these groups, it is to that
end information has been presented. In some cases the presentation
by groupings serves this purpose and can be justified by the following reasons.

a) Those within the grouping are related geographically, perhaps
     intermixed with each other; communication flow may be in the
same direction; or politically they are working together.

b) Origins, customs, religious observances have strong similari-
     ties.

c) Members of the grouping may be occupationally interdependent.

d) Felt needs, frustrations, aspirations form a common bond.

e) One of the group is usually more advanced or progressive and
     shows more response to the gospel. This provides a bridge-
head to reach the others.

f) One of the group is the most influential and thus poses a
     better base for projecting a witness and demonstration
of the gospel.

g) By providing for a clustered approach we may be able to make
     use of a variety of resources and view the project in its
totality.

h) There is at least one potential problem that we need to be
     warned against. A heterogenous approach could slow down the
work. The more homogenous our approach, the less cross-cultural
resistance we will encounter. However, since the work in each of
these tribes, with few exceptions, must be carried out cross
culturally, it is a fact that we must face in any event. Each
homogenous unit should be evangelized as a unit and homogenous
churches formed. Supervision of the work and available resources
may extend more widely.

N.B. New state names are in brackets
        * Target group data sheets occur in same order as they are
        in this section.

1

Plateau State

(Alago / Afo - Bassa - Gade - Gwandara)

Alago

The Alago are centered in Doma, west of the town of Lafia, and to the south and at Keana, Assaikio and Obi. There are some believers in each of these towns. The Basa and Afo are to the west, Benue River on south and Eggon Mada on the north.

Religion and Culture. The hi-god is Oso-Oso, the creator. There are a number of other gods such as Ibaku and Agashu for protection against witchcraft and the idol Abo who assists in prosperity. Others insure health, productivity and fruitfulness. There is a very strong relationship to the ancestors and a family grave is common. The ancestral grave is opened for each new burial. The festival Amiri in November is a memorial for the deceased. Sand is spread at the door of the house, beer is offered, the graves are cleared off and new sand put down. The idol "Odu" keeps the town in safety and prosperity and is worshipped in February/March. This is accompanied by games, dancing and beer drinking. The chief of Doma must first give permission and then each village observes it separately. The Odu youth leader organizes the festival and games. The women's leader, 'sarauniyar mata', gathers the women for the Odu-Isheka. The idol is kept in the center of the town. There is also an annual initiation ceremony for the boys and has to do with the dodo "Agoshi" and "Asuko". An unusual feature of family life is that men often serve the women by farming for them. Women

5

do not farm which is unusual in most animistic societies. Also
the dowry is paid to the mother of the bride. Many Alago women
can be seen daily in the market in Jos selling their cassava flour
although it is over 150 miles from home. There is an independence
here that is seldom seen.

Gospel Penetration. The ECWA work centers in Doma and there are
six local churches in the area. Witness extends to Agwatashi and
Arage and occasional visits as far as the Benue River. A two-year
Bible School is conducted at Doma. Others besides Alago attend.
There are about 180 attending the local church of whom 60 are Alago
people, and nine of these are baptized. Islam has a strong pull
and influence to the Alago. Other important towns are Rutu, Giza
and Aginma.

The EKAS MADA HILLS work in Keana, Obi and Assaikio and report
believers among the Alago in these areas east of Lafia. The
SUM/EKAS conduct a 3-year Bible Training School at Obi which trains
leaders for their entire field.

Readiness to Change. There are indications of deep changes
taking place in attitudes towards the traditional religion. In
some cases when the last elder (baba tsofo) dies all the articles
of worship (tsafi) are buried with him and that is the end of it.
After that it is either Islam or Christianity. Today there is much
greater earning power and a parallel desire for wealth. Youth are
migrating to the cities, particularly Lagos and this is having its
effect upon the group. The Catholics formerly built schools at
Doma and today have a strong following. On balance is the strong
tendency to follow Islam.

Strategy. As noted under culture, women have a strong position
and a high status in the family structure and economy. Perhaps a
greater emphasis upon visiting and winning the household mothers
would yield fruitful results. The local evangelists emphasized
the need for Christians to live among them in their villages so
that the life of Christ in the believer can be seen. The longer
term approach would seem preferable to the aim of getting quick
results since they have shown a resistant attitude in the past.
A good beginning has been made but much more remains to be done.

Afo (Eloyi)

The Afo are southeast of Nasarawa and extend to the Benue River
around Loko being bordered by the Bassa on the west. Other neighbors are the Alago and Gade. They divide themselves into the Hill
Afo and the Plains Afo. The former have been hearing the gospel,
but the latter down towards the river have been neglected.

Culture-Religion. These people are known as being among the most idolatrous of any tribe. One can study this in the Museum in Jos. The hi-god is Ugbo but evidently Adawaji is the father of the land, the most influential in daily practice. Three gods are dedicated to remembrance of the ancestors and regular feasts, sacrifices with beer, are held. The eldest in the clan offers sacrifice to Adawaji. As many as 24 goats may be sacrificed at one time. However, among the Hill Afo the shrines are losing their importance as they observe that the Christians don't need them. Although marriage by exchange was formerly practised, wife stealing, by agreement, is now more common.

Readiness to Change. Education is more prevalent among the Plain Afo and one of their number is a commissioner in Jos. The cultural patterns of marriage and religious observance are changing. Their economic status is improving, and youth are moving off to the cities. Hausa language is spoken by many of them. But the youth generally want to hold on to their traditional dances and worship. This may be due to the influenece of the cultural revival since the Afo have built up a reputation for a highly developed religious culture.

Gospel Penetration. There are seven ECWA churches around the Odegi area and two unorganized groups. In 1974, 21 were baptized. They now have two students at the Karu BTS and another two in local Bible School. They would welcome help from the outside to reach the many towns and villages of the lower valley. The Afo see the Ibo and the Gwandara as being important people. This might be a clue to helping them if Ibo Christian teachers could be encouraged to work among them. Gospel teams have gone as far as Loko but the follow-up has failed. Permanent workers are needed.

Bassa

The population of the Bassa is estimated at 100,000 about ¼ of these being south of the Benue River. The "Kwomu" is supposed to be a derisive nickname. Those south of the Benue originally fled from the Filane warlords of the 19th century. Some reports state that about 29% have become Christian. Another states that only 50% have heard the gospel. Certainly those north of the Benue have held strongly to their traditional beliefs as opposed to either Islam or Christianity.

Religion and Culture. Agwatana is their hi-god and creator but Iglili cares for the people and the village welfare. There is a triennial celebration called Ajuba when the whole village takes part in sacrificial offering of a goat for the protection of the village. Recent attitudes are changing and the traditional cults are dying out. The old men are willing for the children to join Christianity. A Bassa Secondary School student said that youth

are finding out what a real Christian is as opposed to a nominal
one. The cultural revival is finding wide acceptance among the
post primary and university students and this may adversely influence
nominal Christians.

Gospel Penetration. North of Benue: The Qua Iboe have about
25 groups of believers centered on Toto and Umaisha. They operate
two small Bible Schools and dispensaries at Kanyehu and Sardauna.
In the north they absorbed Sardauna and several village churches from
the SIM/ECWA in 1972. There is slow growth, but it is encouraging
recently.

South of Benue: Various Brethren Assemblies are responsible
for majority of the work and Anglican, ECWA and Baptist are beginning to bear fruit. There are some 20 local assemblies and an
estimated 2,000 adherents. The most important matter to watch
here is that harmonious relations may be established among these
various groups. This means respecting one another's Christian
convictions and being willing to cooperate in church planting.

Gade

The Gade occupy an area west of Nasarawa and often live in otherwise Gbari areas but always build their village on the opposite side
of the road. MARC classifies them as a sub-tribe of Gwandara with
population of 5,000, whereas SIL gives 25,000.

Religion and Culture. An annual festival takes place in the
fifth month for blessing upon their farms. Goats and fowls are
sacrificed. The celebration of Usheki, the god of the mountain is
the time for boys and girls to spend some days together. It is
expected the girls will get pregnant. The Gwandara use the same
term for their tree god. An evil person will be buried without
ceremony after first dragging him to the bush, beating him. After
seven days, they cut off his head and give it to the juju priest
in order to atone for his evil. A good person will be supplied
with plenty of beer when he dies. A baby born soon after may have
his spirit.

The marriage pattern is controlled by the parents, and divorce
is unusual. It is tied in closely with certain religious practices
as well as dowry.

Gospel Penetration. The SIM opened work at Ara around 1960,
and the ECWA churches have now increased to eight in the area.
The pastor reports that the Gade in the hills have not yet been
evangelized, and those in the plains near the main roads are
resistant probably due to Islamic influences.

However, it is in between these two areas that there is a response. A few youth are in the Branch Bible School, but at least 10 evangelists could be used right away.

Readiness to Change. Some cultural changes are taking place as more and more they get drawn into the mainstream of events. They see Christianity in a favorable light, although some of them see Islam as being a strong force and are attracted to it. Education is still not popular with them.

Strategy. The Gade are not receptive to the Gbari among whom they live. Hence, it would seem best at first to encourage Gade churches rather than Gade believers worshipping with Gbari. This would help unbelievers to feel more at home and know that Christianity was not just a Gbari thing. At first people need to come to Christ and worship without crossing cultural barriers.

Gwandara

Murdock classifies the Gwandara with the Gade between whom there have always been friendly relations. According to tradition, the Gwandara came from Kano having left there when they refused to become Muslims. Some say that their name, "Gwanda rawa", implies this. In Hausa it means, "it is better to dance". Certainly they have maintained their separate state from Islam as almost 100% are still animistic.

They live in village settlements scattered from Karshi and Karu east to the Eggon Mada near the railway. They are neighbors with the Gbari, Yeskwa, Alago, Gade and Afo, from whom they seem to have borrowed certain customs. There are schools in the area in which they live but few attend. Recently, however, there were five in Keffi secondary, so the situation is improving.

Gospel Penetration. There is no Gwandara church. The few believers meet with their Gbari or other Christian neighbors. The ECWA and Baptists are seeking to evangelize the Gwandara but have met with little success. Their traditional religion is very strong. While walking through one of their villages, I saw numerous large shrines filled with fetishes and sacrificial objects. Every house had a number of fetish charms hanging under eaves and over the door. Youth and children likewise had tied many protective charms around their waist and neck. Witchcraft is very common even to doing away with one's son. When twins are born, special ceremonies with two pots must be put at door of the mother where she first offers any food to be eaten. A black goat and a black fowl must be sacrificed.

Strategy. A resistant people must be approached on a long-term basis with regular recurring visits. Rather than the Gwandara being the object of occasional and sporadic visits and thus a side issue of the evangelist, it will be necessary for someone to take up a ministry among them and devote his full time to it. They all speak Hausa even many words are pronounced similarly to that of Hausa. The objective should be the establishing of a Gwandara church in areas that are showing some response and readiness to change.

2

Kwara State

(Busa - Igbirra)

Busa

To the Busa the high god is a great man, but greater than any
man. He gives rain, fertility and punishes those who do wrong.
Sacrifices of goats and bulls are of great importance. Annual
festivals take place on certain mountains such as Kabak near Wawa.
Death is accompanied by a feast-festival for seven days and
repeated three months later.

It is reported that 90% of the people suffer from guinea worm.
The mother who gives birth to twins is driven away.

Gospel Penetration. The 1964 census showed more than 100,000
people in Borgu Division. The people are variously called Busa,
Boko, Borgu and extend into Benin. SIM (Benin) works among them
at Segbana where the church is being established and there are a
number of village groups. The Methodist have Headquarters at New
Busa. There is a Christian Rural Training Institute at Kaiama.
The former list 25 congregations in 22 locations, most of them
around New Busa and Kaiama. Of the approximate 550 attenders, some
350 are "strangers", i.e. non-Busa people. This leaves about 200
Busa who have made professions of faith. This is probably re-
flected in the attitude of the people toward Christians -- "they
do not count them as anything." Even the pastor has little influence. This may also stem from the fact that among the "stranger"
Christians, there seem to be many who do not live out Christian
principles of honesty, fairness, and love.

An incident illustrates the point. A Busa man was caught
trying to cheat his brother Busa, who then said to him, "Are you
a Yoruba?" They expect Yorubas to try to cheat them. The problem
is they also classify Yorubas as being Christians as they make up
the majority of the "stranger" Christians. However, it is also
exciting to note that the esteemed manager of the CRTI, Michael
Oye is a Yoruba. Everyone respects him highly and recognizes him
as a man of his word. There is need for more like him.

The Methodists have been using teams composed of an agriculturalist, health and literacy personnel and evangelist visiting villages
on a daily basis. They always return to base about 7:00 p.m. Wherea
they have been received very well, the results have been minimal in
terms of interest in the gospel. Perhaps it is because they do not
stay for an evening gathering such as is being done on the Cameroun
border at Gavva where a similar program is yielding large results.

Readiness for Change. Generally there does not seem to be a
readiness for change among the Busa. The strong Muslim influence in
the main towns radiates out to the villages and there is a great
reluctance on the part of the villagers to show interest in the
gospel message. There needs to be more seed sowing and building
of a more positive image of Christianity. The present resources
are inadequate. One pastor is from the Plateau and is a product of
the Faith and Farm movement. "Others of this caliber would be
welcome," said the Methodist missionary, Alan Washbrook. There is
also the need for educated men, more evangelists for the villages
and an increased emphasis upon literacy. Translation into the
vernacular is going forward. Mark is available and soon Luke will
be published.

Some thought should be given to a local dry season Bible School
or a TEE program so that a number of potential leaders could be
trained without taking them away from their livelihood for a
long time.

Igbirra

The Igbirra occupy a triangular area with points at Lokoja, Okene
and Agenebode and across the Niger River in Koton Karfi where they
are often called Kwotto. It is estimated that there are 325,000
in Okene and another 75,000 across the river.

Culture. They are a people with a very strong culture. Their
language is very important to them, but they also use Yoruba.
They continue their annual festivals in spite of the fact that
80% are reckoned to be Muslim and 20% Christian. In other words,
the traditional religion continues to be dominant although the
others are practised overtly.

Two annual festivals are held for nine days each, one in rainy season and the other in December-January. Much is made of masquerade and women are barred from seeing it. Sacrifices are offered to ancestral spirits in order to get prosperity, health, children, and rain. Today each ward has its own masked person representing the ancestor. The great IFA oracle is consulted beforehand to determine who is to be masked and the kind of sacrifice to be offered. The people gather in the towns for these occasions. Otherwise, they spend 10 months of the year living on their farms.

The modern cultural revival movement is having its effect by further encouraging the traditional religion among the youth and students.

Gospel Penetration. By the standards of this study, the Igbirra should be considered as evangelized since 20% are called Christians. Or we should consider them as being Islamized and therefore also outside the scope of this study. However, it appears that the Igbirra are more animistic than either Islamic or Christian. Deep in their hearts there hasn't been much change. The Anglican churches are overflowing, and it is the established church of the area. The ECWA churches are six and quite small. The last few years there has been no growth. The only really dynamic group is the Gospel Assemblies which have small congregations in most villages. Recently the leaders have crossed to Koton-Karfi side and are finding a response there as well. This is probably due to the Assemblies practice of singing, dancing and drumming through the streets and having a more hilarious approach to worship than other Protestant groups. Certainly this is more culturally relevant to the Igbirra. The Assemblies also place a great deal of emphasis on prayer for the sick and healing.

There is a serious dearth of trained leadership from among the Igbirra. ECWA has sent in Yoruba pastors to lead the church. Today there are four untrained leaders, a Grade II teacher, and a seminary trained pastor.

Strategy. There are almost no signs of a readiness to change the status quo and there is evidence that the traditional religion has not lost its vigor. In seeking ways to really reach the Igbirra, perhaps a page should be taken out of the Assemblies book. Can we learn something from them? Should worship meet the felt needs of a people? Is it wrong for people to express their praise to God through drumming, swaying to music, and singing expressively? New converts do not become mature Christians overnight. As they grow in the Lord, they will understand what is best for them. Let's not ask them to cross too many unnecessary cultural barriers before becoming Christians.

3

Kaduna State

(Hausa Maguzawa / Kadara - Koro)

Hausa Maguzawa

There is no real way of knowing how many Maguzawa there are, mixed as they are throughout the areas occupied by the Hausa people. They are as truly Hausa as the ones we describe as Muslim Hausa. Since they turned and ran away from Muslim practices, such as prayers, they were derisively spoken of as "Maguzawa" or "those who ran away". They have occupied an inferior status among the total Hausa nation. However, even in the census reports there is no delineation made between the two groups. But if even 5% were Maguzawa, it would mean there were at least 500,000 (½ million). No one is sure where they are all located scattered throughout the three states, Kaduna, Kano and Sokoto.

Culture. Their outstanding characteristic is family solidarity. It is not unusual to find a "family" of 100 and even up to 500 living as a single unit with a household head whose word is law. They do not speak of their place as a village but as a house (*gida*) and the eldest is not the chief but the father. They have maintained their own ancestral worship and beer drinking is a very strong practice. Maguzawa worship is centered around a shrine of stones covered with a grass roof to which offerings from the farm are brought. Annually there is an offering called "paska" (Passover) which the father offers on behalf of his family. They are very industrious farmers and consider themselves as without peer.

14

Most of them use oxen and raise maize, guinea corn, groundnuts
and cotton. One finds them back away from the main roads and out
of the mainstream of activities. They have a reputation for honesty
and keeping their word. No action can be initiated without the
consent of the father. Even when measuring out grain no one questions their honesty or requests them to measure it in their sight.
Naturally, people like this have been exploited by profiteers.

Gospel Penetration. Three agencies are mainly involved in outreach. The Baptists based in Zaria have begun to reach out to
Gimi, Makarfi and area. The Anglicans based in Wusasa Zaria are
working in a cluster of places 35 miles west of Zaria and about
the same distance to the east near Anchau, and north of Zaria
around Bakori and Rogo. They report 18 organized village churches
with 310 baptized members and many other groups growing into
churches. They need more workers and support for them to provide
leadership--at least two more pastors and seven evangelists. There
is also an evangelist's training school at Wusasa January to
March. In 1975, 13 were trained to teach literacy and other
leaders were given six weeks training in health, evangelism,
taking services and Bible study.

They have been seeking to meet felt needs through an agriculturalist and a health team. These minister in the villages of the
area and have opened many doors. The doctor at Wusasa has taken
over the training of workers and recently 15 men and five women
received instruction in community hygiene. They came from ten
communities. Hospital staff will visit in follow-up.

ECWA has a thriving work farther north centered in Gani,
Sumaila district, Kano State. There are several churches and
other growing points. Another in Gwarzo district and in the
Malumfashi - Matazu area of N.C. State. The pastor told me that
at least 800 gathered at a recent conference in Malumfashi and
there are nine local churches throughout the district. From one
family in Malumfashi, there are now four pastors. This entire
family of 70 persons confessed Christ together a number of years
ago. Leaders told me that over a wide area other households are
ready to take this step. Out from Gusau is another responsive
group of Maguzawa. It seems that wherever a concerted effort
to reach them has been made, that eventually there has been a
response.

Readiness to Change. They do not show many attitudes of change
as usually measured, but circumstances are catching up with them.
There is a strong move to eliminate animistic practices in Nigeria,
and people must confess themselves as Muslim or Christian. They
do not want to become Muslim because of the long history of separation from them. But they do not understand what it means to be
Christian. Universal Primary Education scheme will force them to
put their children in school. In order to do this, they will
have to gather in more centralized locations. Children will
state whether they are Muslim or Christian upon entering school.

Strategy. The ECWA pastor at Malumfashi stated that "within
the next ten years the Maguzawa will make their decision for Christ
or Islam." He further urged that 100 workers be sent into the
harvest field for six months as soon as possible. This would be
an emergency force and would have as their goal the planting of
the church in each place. The pastor believes that his people are
ready to respond now if the message is presented in the right way.

Such an action would require adequate preparation. Where would
workers be found? Perhaps some church leaders and others with
training could leave their posts in the hands of others for this
time. A training course in church planting, discipling new converts
and developing a truly indigenous church should be worked out.
These men would need support for themselves and their family. Where
would they live and to which households would they go? All these
and many other questions need to be answered. But the challenge
is great.

Above all, the important cultural values of this society must
be respected. The father and his brothers and sons need to be
approached first. Since these people are used to acting together,
the evangelist should seek household conversion as Jesus did in
the case of Zacchaeus. The gospel will then travel along family
lines to many other families through the web of relationships.
Such opportunities must be exploited. Every effort should be made
to uncover Maguzawa wherever they are so that every family may be
exposed to the gospel and have opportunity to accept Christ. Literacy is of great importance today. The example the Anglicans
have given us of meeting felt needs should be carefully studied
and applied.

Kadara and Koro

These two groups are culturally and geographically related.
Murdock lists Koro with Kadara. Kajuru-Kufana are Kadara north
and they extend to Adunu on south with Gbari on west. Koro are
to the extreme southern border of N.C. State and extend into
Abuja division of N.W. State where they border with the Kadara on
the north. There is also a section of the Koro (Migili) in Lafiya
division of B.P. State. S.I.L. reports estimate Migili at 10,000,
and the total Koro at around 25,000. Koro are further divided
between *Huntu* in the west around Adunu and the *Zane* in Kagarko
district.

The majority of these people are animistic with some Muslim
infiltration, perhaps 10-15 per cent. The Christian witness has
also begun to penetrate at certain points. A brief summary of
Kadara traditional beliefs is given by S.I.L. (1966):

"They believe in the spirits who dwell in the
trees and in the stones. Ancestor worship is also
prominent. Stones from graves are often carried
inside the house, or if big enough, propped up
against the outside of the doorway. Chains are
often tied around their waists and for three days
in every fourth year there is a beer festival.
The ancestors are believed to appear at this time
and are supposed to be actually seen by those who
have got themselves into the right spirit."

Semi-annually or oftener the dodo Akun is offered beer with
cooked food and meat and left on the stone shrine where the blood
of the animal was sprinkled. In the spring memorials are offered
to the ancestors before farming begins.

Gospel Penetration - Kadara. In the Kujuru-Kufana sector there
are 11 ECWA and eight Baptist local churches, and it is estimated
that 30% of the people would be Christian. In the south around
Adunu (SIM) the work is more recently established, but there are
eight local ECWA churches between Adunu and Kateri.

The unevangelized area is in what may be described as Central
Kadara east of Serikin Pawa and centered upon Doka. It is a very
isolated area and only on occasional treks by missionaries and
evangelists have these people been touched by the gospel. A
motor road is being projected to pass through this country,
and would open the area to evangelization.

Strategy. In the meantime, the church should consider how it
can penetrate this area for Christ. It should be noted that the
Gbaris to the west of Serikin Pawa in Minna division are also
neglected. For this reason, I am suggesting that Adunu could be
used as a staging area for sending evangelists into Central Kadara.
Rural and community development programs are being carried out at
Adunu by the S.I.M. missionary. These ideas could be incor-
porated into an orientation course and thus provide evangelists
with tools for entry into a backward culture. This could become
the supply point for extension.

Rev. Yakubu Yako organized a crash evangelism/church planting
program among the Kuturmis five years ago that has resulted in
a stable work among them. Seven volunteer evangelists supported
by southern Zaria churches went in with the goal to plant churches
within three years. This effort, well planned and directed, proved
very fruitful and effective. A similar move among the central
Kadara might well prove to be the answer.

Koro. The *Huntu* have remained a very remote and backward people living in clearings within dense forest. When a baby is born, it must not fall on its face or else it is cursed and allowed to die in the bush. Twins and babies with a sixth finger are treated similarly. This prompted the S.I.M. (Adunu) to open an orphanage and many babies were saved from death. The orphanage is now entirely operated by the ECWA church and as soon as possible, the children are passed on to reliable Christian parents. There are three local churches among the Koro and several preaching points.

There are signs of change. They are beginning to wear clothing, marriage patterns are modernizing, youth are going off to the cities and even religious observances are undergoing change. Christianity has had a good influence. However, the new converts need teaching and someone to stay with them in their villages. Presently elders of the Adunu church go out weekends to help them with visitation, Bible class and Sunday services. In this way, they encourage a "Paul-Timothy" relationship. Evangelists in this area help the people in use of fertilizer, insecticides, seeds, etc.

In the eastern side of Koro (*Zane*) Kagarko district, there are a dozen or more ECWA churches and some Baptist as well. Their influence reaches to the Gurara River which then acts as a barrier to further outreach except on special ocassions. However, with this base it is reasonable to assume that evangelization and church planting will continue from both east and west until it is complete.

4

Bauchi State

(Miya - Afawa - Buta - Warji / Jarawa - Zaranda Hill People)

Miya - Afawa - Buta - Warji

Excellent descriptions of this group can be read in the ethnographic "Pagan Peoples of the Central Area of Northern Nigeria" by Harold D. Gunn; and in O. Temple's "Notes on the Tribes." Ancestor worship together with sacrifices of bulls and goats accompanied with the spilling of blood on the ancestral shrine is an annual affair. The family 'dodo' is represented by a clump of logs outside each compound. The center post is about three feet high and the surrounding stakes about two feet high. Blood and beer are periodically poured over them and other rites performed. Wrestling is a regular part of every celebration. Great power is attributed to the ancestors, one of whom is the current 'dodo'. It appears that Islam has made a greater impact upon the *Warji* and the *Buta* and particularly the former have adopted Hausa ways. However, as in other tribes, the new religion is more of an overlay and the traditional religious practices and values still keep their hold upon them.

Miya. The *Miya* people have resisted Islam and continue with their traditional festivals centered around sacrifices of dogs. An annual atonement is celebrated every April in which the ancestors are remembered for their blessings of inheritance and life. This is also marriage time and the 'dodo' is responsible for the ceremony. The main festival takes place every four years and is the time for circumcision and other initiation exercises for the boys.

The pastor of the ECWA church, *Miya*, said attendance is over
100 plus perhaps an average of 20 who are on their farms. There
are also four believers in Jimbin. Of the several villages, only
Miya has a church. The people are now beginning to respond more
readily. Besides Miya and Jimbim other related villages are Siri,
Kiriya, Tando, Kafin Zaki, Ganjuwa, Maiwa and Tsagu.

Afawa. The gospel has been proclaimed over the past 40 years
among the *Afawa* but today only one family is considered to be
Christian. Missionaries of S.I.M. resided at Tiffi for a number
of years and trekked throughout the area including that of the Buta
people. Many made professions of faith but it seems that they were
intimidated into believing that it was a false way. Now the elders
testified emphatically that they realize their mistake and they
want help for their people.

Buta. I did not visit among the *Buta* people but a lay evangelist
who spent five years among them reports that Islam has taken over.
These people live on the border of Kano State and are very remote
from the mainstream of life. However, those seeking minerals, the
miners, have long since found the area profitable. May the messen-
gers of the gospel not be too late.

Warji. Katanga is the center of church activity among the *Warji.*
There are six churches in the area and the elders say that nearly
all of the Warji have at least heard the gospel although many haven'
understood it yet. Gospel teams and evangelism campaigns have contributed to the growth of the church. In this group the Warji are
the most progressive and have the strongest body of believers. They
are the key to further evangelization of their own group as well as
of those surrounding them.

A new hospital and school are being built in Ningi. There will
likely be some Christians employed in these institutions. A congregation should be begun in Ningi town as it will serve as a
strong testimony to villagers from Afawa and Buta country that it
is possible to become a Christian and live it.

Gospel team efforts from Warji and Bauchi could work in selected
towns for church planting. Pastors and evangelists could join with
these giving some weeks to evangelizing. Literacy classes in Hausa
should be emphasized.

The E.M.S. of ECWA might consider adding staff in this area. Chri
tian staff of institutions need to be encouraged to help on days off

In all plans it must be remembered that Ningi is a strong center
of Islamic influence. But the people are demonstrating a readiness
for change, and they see Christianity as a favorable option.

In any strategy a strong emphasis should be put upon the Old Testament stories, especially those dealing with sacrifice. The account of Elijah on Mt. Carmel defeating Jezebel's priests demonstrates God's power and that His way of sacrifice is better. One can then build upon this the facts of Jesus Christ and His perfect sacrifice for all men. The Lesson series in this report provides for this kind of teaching. If people can see that your message has some relationship to what they practise, it becomes easier for them to understand and eventually to accept it.

Jarawa

The term includes a large group which extend south of the Jos-Bauchi-Alkalere road to the Plateau border and east to the Geji River. The more important sub-sections are the *Amper* and *Seiyawa* around Lere. They may also be called the *Plains Jarawa*. They were conquered by Bauchi. The *Mbarawa* are in Dass Emirate, *Bankalawa,* and *Jarawa* themselves in Bununu Dass. To the southeast of Bauchi there are the *Duguri* and on their border the *Kanem.* They are strongly influenced by Islam. The *Hill Jarawa* are on the Plateau near Shere Hills whose center is at Fobur. Besides this, there are a number of small groups numbering less than a thousand scattered in pockets of the mountains.

Gospel Penetration. Generally speaking, it appears that the Hill Jarawa are well along in the process of being evangelized. There are 21 organized churches and 57 places of worship. The church at Fobur attracts more than 1,000 for conferences. At least four chiefs are followers of Jesus Christ. The Seiyawa also have responded readily to the gospel and are evangelizing their people in the valley. The EKAS PLATEAU/SUM is responsible for this.

In Dass division, ECWA has eight local churches and another six in Wurno district. In Wandi, Baraza, Lushi, Zumbul, Polchi there are churches but none in Dur. Animists make up 85% with another 10% Muslims. Among the Bankalawa Bajir has no church. Around Gar ECWA has a cluster of three churches among the Duguri people, but growth is very slow.

One pastor called for ten new evangelists and named the towns where they could be located immediately. These included Bazali in Polchi, Dur, Wandi, Bajir, Bazel, Dat, and Dajun. The closer to Bauchi one comes, the greater is the resistance to the gospel.

Religion. The Dodo cult is very important as is the veneration of ancestors who are believed to return at times of feasts and celebrations. The women are kept in deadly fear of the dodo and it is a prime means of husbands keeping women in subjection. There is a five-year festival called the "giyan kasa" (beer festival of the land) at which time all relatives come with sacrificial animals

to the compound of the eldest member. At this time the young boys
go off to the mountain to be initiated into the dodo cult. Age
groups are thus very important. It seems that much of the other
forms of traditional religion are dying out.

There is a Bible Training School at Bayara (ECWA) ten miles
from Bauchi on the Bununu Dass road. There are usually between
60-70 men and their families studying here for four years in preparation for evangelism and church planting throughout the Jarawa
area. Another similar school (ECWA) at Zalanga 50 miles north is
also preparing leaders for new churches. Both of these schools
have students from ECWA and EKAS churches.

Strategy. Some comments from a senior pastor were very helpful.
He said that the *Duguri* and *Kanem* reject the gospel when it comes
to them from the *Angas* and *Seiyawa* people. They consider them as
being very primitive and therefore inferior to them. The Jarawa
have a high opinion of themselves.

In 1975 a Bauchi City evangelism campaign was conducted during
the week of a Muslim sallah (Idal-fitr). All the district heads
and lesser chiefs had assembled for the sallah. A teacher from
Kano openly opposed and tried to disrupt the meetings with his
amplifier. Action was taken by the Liman of Bauchi against this
person, and he was given the choice of either leaving town or
being quiet. He chose to leave. The Liman declared that no one
could attack the Bible. He himself reads it regularly. As a con-
sequence, Bibles were selling so rapidly in Bauchi that distributors
could not keep up. A local bookseller (Muslim) came to S.I.M. Bookshop for more Hausa Bibles. Following this each church district
held its own campaign and found themselves being welcomed by their
rulers. All of which is a message to us that there are open doors
before us today throughout this formerly very difficult area.

The potential resources are there—churches, Bible schools,
believers. How can we mobilize our forces to do the most effective
work? EKAS PLATEAU and ECWA BAUCHI should plan together for joint
outreach sharing each other's goals, weaknesses and strengths.
All spirit of competition and selfishness must be put aside that
we may together glorify only Jesus Christ.

Zaranda Hill People (Geji-Zul-Pelu-Bolu-Girmawa-Dulumi)

These tribes are mainly located north of the Jos-Bauchi road near
the Zaranda Mountain and Nabordo. The reason for looking at them
with Jarawa is geographical and political. It seems that the two
groups should be studied together when consideration is given to
church planting among them.

Gospel. There are small groups of believers (ECWA) at approximately ten mile intervals along the motor road from Toro to Bauchi. But the Christian presence, with the exception of Zul, is not strong. An evangelist has been preaching at Dulumi for seven years (where a fishing festival is held every October) and almost without result. Only they and Pelu have believers among them. For some reason the other people have remained extremely resistant to the gospel. In fact the whole area to the north as far as the Lame-Burra Game Reserve is without any light of the gospel. To the west one must reach the Gumai-Tulu road to find churches and believers. To the east it is the Durum-Miya road before one finds a few Christians.

Culture. These people are almost 100% animistic in their beliefs. The Zaranda mountain is important in their worship for it is from here that they originated. They offer sacrifices and fear the spirits of the forest and mountain. Certain animals such as the crocodile, hartebeest and lion are considered as relatives and cannot be killed on any occasion. There are strong tabus against theft, fighting and murder. Some of the customs such as the large lip and ear discs are being abandoned. With the advent of more primary schools, the young people will be exposed increasingly to the influences of the outside world.

Strategy. A massive effort must be considered by the church. We must put aside comity that allows only a certain group to work in an area. Let us think in terms of the total Church of Jesus Christ. What does Jesus want us to do about these people? What about teams of evangelists-pastors going to strategic towns for 4 - 6 weeks of intensive visitation to lay the groundwork and probe for the responsive areas. Could those in training in the Bible Schools do this as a part of their training. Perhaps the Lord will lead in a completely new pattern. Let us be open to His leading.

5

Borno State

(Babur Thali / Ngamawa)

Babur Thali

They are related to the Babur rulers of Biu Emirate and also the
Burra people to the east of Biu. S.I.L. gives Babur as one of the
alternate names for the Burra and mentions Babur District. The
Babur seem to have split over Islam. The Thali rejected it and
scattered into the bushland northwest of Biu, whereas the Babur
proper remained in control of government under the British and
accepted Islam. It seems there may be a parallel situation here
to that of the Maguzawa Hausa who refused to do 'salla' (Muslim
prayers). They are the agriculturalists and live away from the
mainstream of Hausa society and are regarded as inferior by the
Hausa Muslim. The Burra, being pushed out of Biu around 1900,
welcomed the missionaries and the gospel in the 1920's and today
have a strong church.

Living among the Babur people are remnants of other groups,
sometimes only a single village or a cluster of two or three.
These are known as *Maha, Kimba, Ngulde* and *Shua*. A believer
came from each of these places and gave a brief resume of the
situation, Islam predominates and there are very few believers.

The Kimba, however, are 15 miles north of Shaffa and comprise 11 towns. They are not Muslim but neither are there any Christians. During a New Life for All campaign in 1974, they began to hear the gospel.

Gospel Penetration. Generally it appears that west of Biu along the road to Dadin Kowa where the work joins that of ECWA, there is need for evangelists. Again the area north and northwest of Biu has perhaps three local groups with a few believers in each. During the N.L.F.A. campaign more than a dozen places were visited and the people earnestly begged for further help. There are mosques, but they are only used during the month of fast. The people worship their gods in the forms of trees, stones and shrines.

Culture. Their families are very important to them, and they value hard currency above anything else. Society is changing, however, and marriage is not as stable as formerly. There is a great need for clinics, health care and agricultural assistance. Youth no longer consider the traditional religion with favor.

Strategy. Here then is an area of perhaps 50,000 to 75,000 people who are strongly influenced by Islam through political, religious and economic pressures. The Burra Bible is available, and they understand Hausa well. To the north and east are the Kanuri and Beriberi. The few contacts in recent years have drawn a favorable response. Closest to this situation is the EKAS LARDIN GABAS/CBM church, and on the western border is ECWA Gombe District. This is a frontier situation that demands courage, vision and prayerful planning by all concerned.

Ngamawa (Ngamo Gamawa)

The Ngamo are a sub-group of the Karekare and according to S.I.L., may number as high as 18,000. They spread out north of the Gongola River and spill over into Gombe and Darazo districts. The mountain at Gadaka is the traditional site of origin. They claim to have preceded the Bolewa who now exercise authority in the district. SIM/ECWA is working out from Gadaka with district headquarters in Potiskum. It is said that the Catholics are making rapid progress particularly through use of reading classes.

Culture. Whereas the Karekare have largely succumbed to Islamic influences, the Ngamo have remained in their animistic tradition. Their creator is N'deyi na Ako, who is their ruler and "there is no one greater." They celebrate 'kamti' every three years with the sacrifice of a goat. The god gives fertility to animals as well as women and helps in the birth of a child. Angels are said to

care for each home and a ceremony is carried out each week. The
offering is first given to N'deyi and then thrown away. They also
have a tradition about a flood that swallowed up all the people.

The most important thing for them is the matter of security for
the future. One wife is the norm. Children are important in their
value system as they offer the security they seek. Two weeks following death, the deceased will commune with the living relatives
during a special ceremony. A barren woman at this time will go
to the grave so that she may be restored to childbearing.

There is an annual feast when all the guilt of the house is
placed on an animal that is sacrificed. A kind of atonement day.
The shedding of blood is of great importance as well as the offering of food at appropriate times, such as first fruits and harvest
time.

Strategy. Generally the informants divided the unit into three
geographical areas. The sandy areas of the valley border to Bauchi
Division and the Denawa people have been resistant to the gospel.
In the Gudi-Gadaka area, there are perhaps 80 believers. And
another 30 in the Janga area. A list of the major towns where
there is no permanent witness gives an idea of the size of the
remaining task.

The larger towns: Gudeli, Jigawa, Gidan Aba, Gidan Doya,
                   Kafa Ali, Kiyayo, Shinge, Kuli, Nahuta,
                   Garkuwa, Turmi, Maluri, Kurmi, Dadin Kowa,
                   Gidan Ganji.

There are believers in Gadaka, Kusami, Gadana, Dufuel (to
the east) and Catholics mainly in Mincika. The ECWA church among
the Karekare is mainly responsible for the Ngamawa work. A Bible
school at Kukar Gadu (ECWA) has supplied several evangelists but
there is a great lack of workers to spearhead an outreach into
these remaining towns. With the increase in educational facilities
and the increased need for teachers, we may find that new opportunities will open up. Gospel teams from Potiskum-Kukar Gadu
area could also make an impact that would result in new groups of
believers. The whole area is neglected and the people would benefit
from health care, medical help, literacy and better ways of farming
and raising poultry and animals. See the report on Babur Thali which
is southeast of the Ngamo people.

6

Gongola State

(Mandara Mountains / Fali / Vere / Mumuye / Daka - Jibu - Ndoro)

Mandara Mountain People

The proliferation of tribal groups here seems to be almost endless.
S.I.L. has very carefully sorted them out and shown the equivalent
of the various names used. Here I will use those that seem to be
in common use, both in the area concerned and by those who have
studied the groups. Information given is not complete, but hope-
fully it will be such that our minds will begin to grasp the complexity of the task, and we will be challenged to intensive action
on behalf of these people.

    The Groups: Dghwede, Glavda, Guduf, (Gava) Zladivha,
                  Hidkala, Matakam, Ngoshe Ndahang (Sama), Sukur,
                  Tur, Vemgo (Waga).

The Mandara are excluded because of their being Islamized
according to reports. The last three are in the Madagali district,
but the others are in Gwoza district. The mountains run roughly
north and south paralleling the Cameroon border. At the northern
end, a gently rolling plain extends from the base of the mountain
to the border. Further south the plain is swallowed by the mountains.
All of these groups inhabited the mountains at one time, but today
some members are coming down into the valley on either side. Gwoza
is a melting pot and a score of tribes can be found represented
in the market each week. Those who want change and are willing to
experiment with life on the outside of their cultural boundaries

have come down. Hence they are more open to the message of the
gospel. Those remaining in the hills are usually tradition-bound
and quite resistant to the gospel.

The *Hidkala* and their relatives inhabit the valley on the western
side from Madagali to Gwoza along the motor road. There are several
churches here and farther west among the Marghi. One can reach the
Dghwede, Glavda, Gava, and *Zladivha* by the motor road from Pulka
that follows the eastern slope. The *Matakam* live mainly in the
Cameroon and have a strong Christian element there. They are traditional enemies with the *Dghwede*. Ngoshe is difficult of access
but can be reached by motor through the Cameroon or by foot from
Limankara. The *Sukur, Tur, Vemgo* are being reached from Gulak,
a Basel Mission Station.

Religion/Culture. Most of these groups indicate a similar
origin and many customs have a common background. Every compound
has a bull/cow house where the animal is tethered continually for
three years. The tall post to which the animal is tied for slaughter-
ing is very conspicuous as it stands above the surrounding houses.
Since a new one is put in place every three years, one can tell when
a family is going to offer its triennial sacrifice. At this time
all the members of the family return home. There is great feasting,
beer drinking and revelry. The Guduf men particularly are greatly
addicted to drinking often beginning early in the morning. The
women approve of this because it is a source of income for them.

At Sukur the eighth baby used to be killed. Now it is given
to a Fulani. Blacksmiths constitute a low class clan and do not
intermarry with others. People will leave a hoe for repair at the
gate. Fetishes include pots in trees and sticks laid in patterns
on paths. At the entrance to Sukur a goat or sheep skin hangs
across the path to stop any sickness from entering. The chief has
a juju house in a big rock, which only he can enter (SIL). There
are no Sukur Muslims and only a few Christians but none are baptized.

The Dghwede make a great deal of ancestor worship. It was
reported that there are ten gods and three ancestral shrines and
that animal blood sacrifices are very important to them. Blood
is rubbed on the door of the eldest. Beer is causing so much
trouble through fights that many want medicine (power) over it.

Among the Guduf there is a family shrine with stones where each
member sits. The family gathers annually and the eldest will spill
the blood of the sacrifice on the altar. Much beer is drunk and
the blessings of "Yashgila" the high god are invoked.

Farming. Grain is not only important for food but also for
beer. The mountain slopes are cleverly terraced and the farms are
interspersed with the rocks. It is an incredible accomplishment.
The women do most of the farming. Most people prefer life on the
mountain because of the "air and water."

Evangelism and Church Planting. About 20 years ago the S.U.M.
Plateau opened a hospital at Gwoza. Dr. Chandler used it as a
base for evangelism as well. By this means many of these tribes
people first heard the gospel. Workers would use free time climbing the mountains and witnessing. The EKAS PLATEAU cooperated by
sending in missionaries and the church was planted at several
points along the motor road - Pulka, Uvaha, Gwoza, Limankara - as
well as to the west 25-30 miles. Today there is an evangelist among
the Guduf on the mountain and another at Ngoshe where a dispensary
has been opened also. There is a strong church at Pulka with an
experienced pastor and a Bible School at Limankara. The hospital
has been taken over by the Northeast State government. The S.U.M.
maintain a missionary couple at Limankara.

The Church of the Brethren and EKAS Lardin Gabas extends to
Madagali. Today the church has joined with the Basel Mission in
the work at Gulak and also at Gava on the eastern side opposite
Gwoza. At Gava there is a 36-bed hospital and a dozen churches
with trained leaders. Besides the Gava-Guduf they are reaching the
Glavuda and the Dghwede people. The medical ministry has given
them a strong base of operation and they are seeking to increase
the size of it. A medical team regularly hold clinics in selected
towns and this has greatly increased the effective outreach.

Teams composed of an evangelist, agriculturalist, nurse and
literacy worker spend four days in a town that is marked for church
planting. They minister to the needs of the people during the day
and in the evening gather for a service of singing, testimony,
drama and proclamation of the gospel. This has been eminently
successful and more than 500 were added to the church last year.

Down at Gulak a similar type work is being carried out. Basel
missionaries are heading this up with the help of EKAS evangelists
and pastors. The Sukur kingdom is 15-20 miles east and they report
a congregation of over 50 and three other points with believers.
The Sukur are being urged to descend but so far they have resisted.
However, they are now requesting a school. Twenty years ago they
forced the school to close by boycotting the teacher.

The church at Gulak, although large with 450 members, is not
zealous in witness. A coldness has settled in, and discipline
is slack. As Muslim influence increases, some Christians want
the honor of it. Among the Vemgo (WAGA) there are about 30 scattered believers. Bebel is the center of Islamic influence and there
is an L.E.A. school. The Fulani language is the trade language.

The missionary pointed out that ten evangelists could be used
right away. But they would have to be men with a deep commitment ready to serve the Lord in difficult places. In resume, it

would seem that there are four strategic points in this area:

1) *Gava* with its hospital and strong team approach to church planting.

2) *Pulka* an anchor point at the north end and strategically placed to reach other groups.

3) *Gwoza-Limankara* has a line of churches along the highway and a Bible School for training leaders for new churches.

4) *Gulak* center for southern end of this area and base for the work.

Midling and Midlo are centers of influence. With these bases already established it is a matter of further concentration and expansion until all of these tribal groups have understood the gospel. Anyone working in these mountains should not overlook the S.I.L. reports of 1966, 1970 and 1973. Areas are well defined and culture is described.

The 1963 census figures show the following for Gwoza N.A. district. Hidkala and Zladivha = 2,513 Margi = 10,804 Glavda = 19,353 Guduf = 21,313 Dghwede = 18,853 Ngoshe = 2,513. In addition the Sukur is estimated 10,000; Vemgo 3,000; Tur 2,300 = Total 120,000.

The only scripture translation is the New Testament into Matakam and it is not being used (SIL Ngoshe 1970). Work is in progress on Dghwede, and a few stories from Mark are completed. Primers are in draft stage (1973).

Readiness to Change. The majority are still living as they have for centuries. The few who have left their ancestral homes and moved off the mountain are integrating into new societies. Their children will begin to go to school, and they are being exposed to new influences. These will gradually filter back into the ancestral areas. The evangelist is an instrument of change also, but he must be very patient in the face of this strong traditional history. For example, among the hill Guduf after five years of witness, there are only three young men who have believed. There are 30, however, in the little church at the base of the mountains. Generally the influence of Christianity has been favorable. They want nothing to do with Islam. At Ngoshe Sama there are now 17 believers, and it is growing.

It seems that only the youth and younger adult men hear Hausa or Fulani which are the trade languages. However, with the insistence of the government that the people come down to the plains,

there will be an increased use of these languages. For this
reason there are differing opinions as to what to do about translation into tribal languages. Hausa is usually used and inter-
preted as necessary.

Strategy for Evangelism. In the resume some suggestions were
made. The evangelistic community development team and the village
clinic approach meet definite felt needs. One thing that was
mentioned frequently was the availability of water and the lack of
it in the plains. Is there something we could do here? Literacy
for the youth is highly desirable, and will become increasingly
important. The presentation of the gospel must begin with
the stories of the Old Testament to which they can relate very
readily. With their strong emphasis on animal sacrifice and the
gathering of the clan, one can speak with confidence about Abraham
and Isaac, the Passover Lamb, and Elijah on Mt. Carmel. See the
suggestions on Steps to Evangelism and Church Planting.

Fali

The Fali are the near neighbors of the Higi to the north and the
Gude on the south. The Higi have experienced a tremendous people's
movement and this is beginning to spread into the Fali tribe where
there are now 61 small groups of believers (EKAS GABAS). It is important to note that there is likewise a turning to Christ among
the Gude. In December, 1973, S.I.L. reports there are 2,000 Christians and half a dozen different groups working among them. From
this it appears that a definite work of the Holy Spirit is taking
place all along this mountainous country bordering the Cameroons,
where each of these units also have large numbers of people. It
is for these reasons that this report deals only briefly with one
of these units, the Fali.

Religion. Although the Fali believe in a high-god who is the
creator, their worship centers around the spirits that inhabit the
rocks, hills, trees. Sorcery is greatly feared, and death is
usually attributed to it. Sacrifices are especially offered at
the death of a father. His spirit returns and the family has
communion with him. Each household acts as a unit in such worship.

Culture. Marriage is very unstable, wives changing husbands
and husbands taking new wives indiscriminately. The Christian
leaders feel that there is generally a very low regard for women.

Their farms are worn out and a desire for agricultural help is
indicated. Health and medical care can only be obtained in centers
such as Mubi or in a church/mission clinic. Parents are still
hindering their children from going to school. Although the youth

are strongly in favor of the cultural revival presently taking place in Nigeria, other customs such as child bethrothal have generally ceased.

Readiness to Change. On the scale of readiness to change, the Fali do not have a high score. The influence of Christianity, however, has been excellent, and the people prefer it to Islam with which they associate the rulers of their district. It is encouraging to see that three leaders have finished the Kulp Bible School and that two others are in the advanced course. It was reported that the Catholics have had no success during the 15 to 20 years they have been working there.

It would appear, therefore that every effort should be made at this time to pursue the evangelization of this tribe to its fringes. The harvest is ripe. The work has begun well.

Vere

There are several sub-sections of the Vere such as Koma (about ½ of total) Vomni, Samlo, Sardi (later two live on plain), Wongi and Zagai (mountains). The Koma and Vomni have been most responsive but work has also been begun in the others. Gurnati is the main Christian center for 36 local churches. Each has an evangelist in charge, some of whom have had Bible School training.

Religion. Those living in remote mountainous areas have shown little inclination to change and the gospel has not yet penetrated to them. The Vere are idol worshippers and believe in spirits that inhabit the mountains and forests. They offer innumerable sacrifices of grain, beer and goats to the cult of "dodo". The dodo cult is an elite group who have given particularly large offerings and thus gone through a series of grades over a period of years. One of the informants (now a Christian) had reached the senior level and was known as "Da'os". This person is then allowed to cover himself with a large cowhide which symbolizes to all the importance of his position. This is quite a different concept from the 'dodo' of central Nigeria.

Legend tells of the high-god Bilapel who created man and gave him a position of great honor. However, some men did not obey him. Sacrifices of dog and food were offered and those who had been obedient prayed. Nevertheless a drum fell from heaven and death ensued. This accounts for the beginning of sin and death.

When someone is caught thieving, grass is tied to his hand and it is set on fire. Although it is controlled, the purpose is to inflict a scar for life so that the thief will fear punishment of eternal fire, in which they also believe. In most of our studies, we did not find a belief in eternal punishment.

Both of the above accounts provide opportunity for giving the biblical truth and to show that there is no need to fear death in Jesus Christ.

Felt Needs. Agriculture is considered very important because of the large quantities of food required by the dodo cult. Only a few oxen are being used but the Christians have begun to use 'takin zamani' (fertilizer). Health care is a vital concern as well as adequate supply of water for daily needs.

Readiness to Change. Traditional cultural patterns are beginning to change. Children going to school, patterns of betrothal are changing, new agricultural crops such as guavas and bananas are being introduced. This is in turn bringing about chang es in standards of living. The influence of Christianity is rated very high. When the pastor was queried as to the most important need of the believers, he cited the problem of lack of faithful stewardship. It seems that when people become Christian they were relieved of the heavy burden put on them by the dodo cult, and they didn't see the value nor the purpose of giving to the Lord. The church leaders are seeking to correct this problem with teaching.

The Lutheran Church of Christ (EKAS) is the only Protestant group working among this people. It seems that an excellent beginning has been made and that with continued emphasis upon evangelism and church planting, every village and hamlet will have opportunity to know the Lord. This, of course, must be accompanied with a corresponding discipling and teaching program in each local church.

Mumuye

Religion. Temple describes a typical worship ceremony. "Wuka" is the principal god, the god of fate. Women may not even hear of him, and the elders alone may see his effigy, a featureless mask of red wood with two horns and a protruding mouth in the center. 'Donso' is consulted as to death, but is not considered infallible. 'Aku' presides over trials by ordeal--a horn is blown before he speaks. Here are many wooden images, some two feet high, representing both sexes" (Temple 290).

Gospel Penetration. The population figures vary from 120,000 to 250,000. It probably depends on whether certain fringe groups are included. However, most seem to agree that some 200,000 people are involved. Animism strongly predominates with some Muslims. Christianity has taken hold around Zing where there are 19 local groups of believers in seven organized churches. In addition, there are a few groups along the motor road from Jalingo to Beli.

The EKAS MURI pastor at Jalingo told us that there were large areas of Mumuye that are unreached with the gospel. He emphasized that there were no Christians, no witness, no plan

and no one to do it. This included the area from the Benue
River east across the motor road and on into the mountains
bordering with the Chamba. It is difficult to assess how many
people are involved, but it would appear to be a large proportion
of Mumuye.

Strategy. Historically the SUM/METHODIST with the EKAS
MURI church have been responsible for the work among the Mumuye.
Unfortunately, within the last ten years there has been a serious
break in relations within the church. Among other things, this has
affected the outreach of the church. There is no longer any heart
nor strength left for this high priority. Prayer and patience is
needed that this situation may be settled. Pastor Siman Jatutu
of EKAS Jalingo reported to the N.E.F. consultation in March 1976
that this serious break in relations had been restored and that
unity and fellowship once again prevailed. We rejoice in this
evidence of the Holy Spirit's working in hearts. In the meantime,
we cannot stand idly by and let these people continue in darkness.
As indicated already, the neighboring sister churches could counsel
together with this church and find a way to complete the evangelization of this great people.

Daka - Jibu - Ndoro

This group is a geographic cluster and is administered from Gembu,
Mambilla division. The SUM/CRC / EKAS BENUE mission/church are
the only group to plant churches among them. The people also
exhibit a strong matrilineal tendency in inheritance patterns and
matrilocality for newly married couples. Traditional religion continues to be very strong throughout the area. Islam is a strong
influence politically and economically, yet the people are not
enamored with becoming adherents.

It is reported that the people prefer Christianity. For example,
recently the Christmas celebrations came at the same time as the
Sallah and the courtyard at Serti was deserted. Most people preferred to observe the Christian's holiday. Where the gospel is
just getting a foothold among the *Daka* across the Taraba River
the people still fear reprisal and therefore give the evangelist a
reserved welcome. The *Ndoro* give the 'boka' VIP status. It
appears that the position of chief priest may either be inherited
or bought if you have the price.

The Bible School at Baissa serves the churches of this group.
It is good to note that there are four from Daka, two from Jibu,
as well as a number from Ndoro. In addition to this, an elementary
Bible School is conducted at Serti. Training such as this in the
early stages of the work will result in good leadership and a
stable church. It also provides for constant expansion.

Strategy. In fact there is a need for three sister groups, EKAS MURI, EKAS BENUE, EKAS LUTHERAN, to study the areas and the people where the normal boundaries of their work come together. There is a tendency to both overlap and overlook otherwise.

The *Daka* are unfortunately partially blocked out from the normal flow of communication by the Taraba River. It is a mighty rushing torrent for much of the year and is difficult to cross. They have been left in the hinterland behind nature's barrier. The *Chamba* people with whom they are related communicate in the other direction eastward and north both for government and church life. The *Mumuye* to the north of the Daka are themselves largely unevangelized. A special concentrated effort will be needed to bring the light of the gospel to them with some impact.

Traditional religion is deeply rooted in their most important annual festival. It lasts for ten days and involves the whole town. Two sacred idols, male and female, are kept secretly in the mountain some distance away. These gods represent the origin of the Daka people. Annually they are brought out by the elders and a parade is formed. The idols are carried from house to house in greeting and blessing of the household. In another ceremony a ram is slain in place of a man thus saving his life from the death by sorcery.

Both of these ceremonies give a good basis for witness to what God has done for man in this world. One can see glimmers of light. Surely at one time man knew God but darkness overtook him.

The felt needs of the *Daka* are very many indeed. Literacy, medical clinics, roads, schools, agricultural help are greatly needed. Greatest of all is for people who really care for them and show love of Christ.

W.B.T. states that *Daka* (Dirim) language is related to Chamba. Since there is a strong Chamba church, it might be well for them to consider outreach into the Daka people. The Chamba church has been organized by the EKAS LUTHERAN with headquarters in Numan.

The *Jibu* are cousins of the Jukun and it is good to note that the Kuteb (Jukun) are assisting in the church planting. One would like to encourage this kind of sharing across ethnic lines so that the strengths of one group may be made available to those that are still struggling. This is the spirit of the New Testament churches. There are now nine Jibu in the Serti Bible School training for leadership. The tape cassette has been a productive tool. Jibu tunes for gospel songs and preaching in Jibu has attracted many listeners and they seem to remember what they hear. There is a need for more players so that this work can be extended.

Ndoro now has two organized churches with at least ten preaching points. It is mostly the youth who are becoming Christians. Those back in the hills are very slow to change. Lay members are going out in pairs to the villages on Sundays. The fact that Christians are making an impact is seen in that many non-Christian villagers no longer farm on Sunday. Now that changes are taking place and believers are looked upon favorably, we need to find ways to move in with great strength and completely evangelize these people. Be sure to look carefully at the section on Suggested Steps for Evangelism and Church Planting.

7

Niger State

(Kambari - Duka - Fakai - Achipa / Kamuku - Gbari)

Kambari - Duka - Fakai - Achipa (Kontogora Division)

Within this geo-political area, there are two other major groups. The *GUNGA* are fishermen and farmers living along the Niger River and under the Emir of Yauri. It is reported that they are Islamized and there are no Christians among them. The *DAKARKARI* are a tribe of some 60,000 with administrative center at Zuru and there is an aggressive UMCA/UMS work with several local churches in their midst. They are also assisting in the evangelizing of the DUKA and FAKAI tribes. It was not felt necessary to describe them as a frontier situation as they have the potential to continue outreach to the fringes of their people.

Kambari

According to Temple, it is probable that the Kambari are descendants of the Atsifawa (Achipa) and Katsina tribes, and they still preserve a close connection with the Katsinawa. Also in common with the Dakarkari, Atsifawa and Bangawa (S. Dakarkari) they carry loads on their shoulders. (Gbari to the east do the same). In common with the Bassa and Kamuku the Kambari worship the god "Maigiro," but the practice is not invariable.

Playmates of the Kambari are the Dakarkari, Katsina, and Beri Beri.

Religion. There are at least seven district subdivisions to the tribe and worship forms and names of gods vary considerably. However, Maigiro is apparently widespread and very important. The Maigiro cult uses a particular hollow tree for a drum and a whistle or flute is blown from the tree top. During a seven-day period, the youth are initiated and much feasting takes place. No woman is allowed outside during this time. At the end of this time, the Maigiro is believed to go up to the sky.

Readiness to Change. It is significant that in 1975 at Salka, a traditional Kambari stronghold, that a serious fight took place in which blood was shed over the continuance of this worship. The result is that it has been banned by the elders thus leaving a definite vacuum in their religious belief and practices. Consequent to this, a group of Muslim teachers attempted to introduce Islam, but were driven off by the townspeople. Recently there have been an increasing number of professions of faith in Christ. The people say that Christianity is preferable to Islam.

Gospel Penetration. Salka is the center of Christian witness and in the area, there are nine Kambari pastors. However, there are not any Kambari students in training in the Salka Bible School presently. New Life for All helped to mobilize believers for witness and had a good effect. Camps are conducted for 5 - 8 days around Salka mainly for fellowship and revival of believers. But evangelistic activities also take place in the nearby communities.

It is apparent that the gospel has not reached very far from main centers. On the Agwarra side of the Niger (Kwara State), there is an estimated 60,000 people with a wide open door. The Emir has urged them to preach recognizing the moral value of Christianity. He has also appointed a pastor to the Welfare Committee. The triangle drawn between Kontagora, Rijau and Yelwa has hardly been penetrated by the church.

Strategy. The Kambari occupy an important position in western Nigeria. Because of their large number, skills and aggressiveness, they wield much influence upon their neighbors. They also have cordial relations with other important groups such as the Katsina and Beri Beri who are behind the barrier of Islam. In addition to this, there is a new openness among them to change. Another factor is the activity of Christians in the army barracks at Kontogora. About 40 have been undertaking house-to-house visitation throughout Kontogora on Saturdays. This is a new and effective voice for the gospel. The local believers are very few and in all the years have never been able to do this. To date, the only witness in this area has been the UMCA/UMS plus the Baptist Mission which operated a hospital at Kontagora until it was taken over by N.W. State a few years ago.

This leads me to suggest that the KAMBARI are the strategic people in this area upon which to concentrate our efforts in the immediate future. It may be that other denominations could contribute of their resources. In another section of this report, steps are outlined for evangelism and church planting. This large ethnic group offers an excellent opportunity for a multimedia approach using radio, literacy aids, literature, cassettes, phonographs, and posters. Such an intensive effort would result in stepped up activity and interest among the Duka, Fakai, Achipa and Busa.

Duka

The largest church among the Duka people is Tungan Magajiya but the attenders are largely Dakarkari who have come in for employment. The Duka have been slow to respond. Two U.M.S. missionaries are leading an effort to produce literacy materials in the Duka language with the help of a national. However, there is not general agreement that this is worthwhile. So far the Duka people have not shown a great interest in it. The question is would materials in the vernacular help to awaken these people to their need of Christ? Or do they see Hausa as being more important to them, and therefore have no motivation to learn their own language. There appears to be a high degree of readiness for change and Christianity is preferred to Islam. Perhaps gospel teams of Kambari youth could help plant churches in a number of villages.

Fakai

Education is coming in slowly. They do not hear the other languages around them and not all use Hausa. The Maigiro system is very widespread. The UMCA/UMS have reached out from Zuru and there are two churches with pastors. Christians are less than 100. It should be noted that the *Dankarkarki* believers are reaching out to the groups on their borders. They are definitely a key to further expansion in this area, which includes the DUKA, FAKAI, ACHIPA.

Achipa

This is a little known tribe of about 2,500 that lives in great isolation in a remote area and have little contact with outsiders. The tribe has remained pagan. Only one young person has been known to make a profession in Christ. There are no schools.

The Achipa have two chiefs, one who is an administrator and another who is their god. (The latter is reported to be purposely blinded for life). The god-chief is never seen by his worshippers and communication with him must be through an intermediary. A New Life for All team visited them briefly in March 1966 (WBT 1970). Reports suggest that outsiders would be resisted. United prayer is the best strategy for the present.

Kumuku - Gbari (Minna Division)

The Kamuku inhabit the area generally between the Gbari on the
east and the Kambari on the west. Their origin seems to coincide
with that of the Kambari and Duka in Katsina. They have good
relations with the Maguzawa and the men of Zaria (Temple). However, circumstances forced them close to the Gbari and today most
of the people are included in the Minna division. They are also
found as far west as Kontonkoro where certain customs bear strong
resemblance to that of the Kambari, e.g. wrestling and Maigiro
cult.

The Pongo, Baushi, Ura and Ngwe (Ngwoi) are included with the
Kamuku and Makangara Kamuku. See the map for distribution.

The Maigiro cult seems to be the strongest daily influence in
their religious experience. Worship of the high god is rendered
through the Maigiro priest. "Everywhere there seem to be rituals,
involving beer drinking, feasting, and the appearance of masked
spirits, at planting, at the height of the rains, in anticipation
of the harvest, again at harvest time, and--the major manifestation
of Maigiro--at the height of the dry season" (Peoples of the
Middle Niger).

Gospel Penetration. Rev. Tuller, independent missionary,
worked in Uregi in the 1940-50 decades but left no organized
church. ECWA has a church and dispensary in Tegina which now is
a part of a cluster of three local churches and is growing slowly.
The Baptist from Kaduna began an organized church in 1959 at
Pandogari and now have eight congregations with 400 adherents at
strategic points along the road. They report slow growth. At
Kakangi deep in the bush, a group of believers was started through
the gospel teams of New Life for All in 1965. The Baptist nurtured
this work for five years, but there is no leader there today.

The Baptist pastor at Kagara reported interference by the local
district head so that believers feared meeting together without
his permission. The pastor has taken this up with him but so
far there is no change.

Strategy. The Baptists are making strategic use of their studen
from the Kawo Bible Training School (Kaduna). During the time of
our interview, several students were being located at new points of
growth for a month of teaching and preaching. This kind of sup-
plementary program strengthens the hands of the pastors and
evangelists.

The ECWA churches around Tegina are related to ECWA Gbari
organizationally, with their district office in Abuja. In both
cases the lines of communication are very long and separate. Could

there be some joint planning on how to best complete the evangelization of the Kamuku people? There is also the possibility of
driving a wedge into the Kamuku from Kontonkoro side.

Let us also be alert to the developments associated with U.P.E.
and gain the help of any Christian teachers posted to remote places.
Although the Kamuku have been resistant until recently, recent
developments in the country are helping to break people loose from
their traditional ways and reluctance to change. There must be ways
that we could meet certain deep felt needs for progress through
literacy, health care, and agriculture. For further suggestions,
see the section on Suggested Steps for Evangelism and Church
Planting.

Gbari Yamma

The Gbari Yamma are an important sub-section of the Gbari group
and are distributed from Kwangoma in the north, down the east half
of the province to Paiko and Lapai in the south. The important
towns are Paiko, Guni, Fuka, Gini, Kuta, Galadima, Kogo, Birnin
Gwari, Guna, Maikonkelli, Bosso and Minna. According to one
authority, there are some five to eight dialects represented in
this group. The Gbari women carry loads on their shoulders as do
the Kamuku and Kambari and it is believed there may have been a
common origin. The Maigiro cult is very strong in each of these
groups also.

Religion. Temple states that the Gbari believe that their
ancestors are born again into some subsequent generation and that
the dead influence the welfare of the living. Each man worships
the spirit of his grandfather, hence the rejoicing at the death of
an old man, who is now able to protect the interests of his grand-
children in the spirit world, of which Maigiro is the early director
and representative or priest.

Each individual male Gbari Yamma worships a personal god, or
guardian spirit, whose shrine is in a special tree in the forest
where offerings of fowls and beer are made. Should a man fall
sick a member of his family goes to the tree of his spirit and
prays for his recovery.

In Kuta, the supreme god is known as Sheshu or Soko, but as in
the case in most tribes, he is too great to take an active interest
in them, so they do not worship him but devote themselves to offering sacrifices to Maigiro. The latter god can prevent crops from
maturing, bring disease, and cause persons to be bewitched. No
woman may be present during the carrying out of rites as it could
result in death or barrenness.

Gospel Presentation. Gospel work was first opened by S.I.M. in Minna, Paiko and Izom. Minna is a typical city situation with substantial congregations composed largely of "strangers". In Kuta, there are eight local churches throughout the district. Considering the span of time since the introduction of the gospel (1910) one realizes how resistant these people have been. Islam exerts a strong influence upon them. By contrast, the eastern half of the tribe, Gbari Matai, has been very responsive. ECWA now has more than 100 churches and over 10,000 in attendance. Baptists also have some churches.

One reason advanced for this resistant attitude was that some of the early leaders in the founding of the church later turned to Islam and this has had a continuing detrimental effect upon further response.

The Baptists have their main church in Minna and a scattering of small groups throughout the area. No statistics were available.

The New Testament has been published but very few are interested in it. Hausa language is important to the Gbari so that he can cope with political and economic situations. If he is going to become literate, there is strong motivation toward Hausa.

Unevangelized Area. From Zungeru to Serikin Pawa and north to Kaduna and Kushaka, there is very little gospel witness being carried on. The area is remote and difficult of access. Both Baptists and ECWA are working on the fringes of the area but a concerted, intensive effort is needed today if these people are to have a fair opportunity to accept Jesus Christ. There is some evidence of readiness to change. Youth are migrating to the centers; marriage patterns are changing and people are looking for a higher standard of living. In the last ten years, the response in the Kuta area has been very encouraging.

The Gbari have given prominence to animal sacrifices and oblations of beer in their traditional religion. The former can become the basis for introducing accounts of such from the Old Testament that naturally lead on to Christ. There is a great need for medical and health care. Farming is their chief occupation and means of livelihood. Hence efforts to improve their crop yield should prove fruitful as well as gaining their confidence. Consult the section on Steps to Evangelism and Church Planting for further suggestions. The area is large and careful survey should be carried out to determine where new work could be best begun. Would it be possible for leaders of the Baptist and ECWA groups to work together in this? The strong Gbari Matai churches form a natural reservoir of potential manpower for the evangelization of the Yamma group. Also the large ECWA Diko church is organizationally linked with the Yamma. Kuta, Serikin Pawa, Gwagwada, Pandogari=Alawa, and Kushaka are possible staging points for a new advance.

8

Marginal Groups Not Included In This Report

Although the groups listed below are included in the MARC Unreached People's File and in Barret's Frontier Situations, there is ample reason to believe that today the situation has changed sufficiently as to not warrant including them in these categories. There is a sufficiently strong Christian witness within the group to warrant believing that they will continue to evangelize their people to the fringes.

Ankwe

The Ankwe proper around Shendam are very largely Roman Catholic and from that standpoint still in need of the gospel. The people however would call themselves Christian. Surrounding the Ankwe (and often included under their name) are a number of smaller tribes in the hills. After talking at length with the pastors and evangelists I am convinced they have the task in hand.

Bunu

They are a branch of the Yoruba. Both the Anglican and ECWA are working among them and report strong churches.

Mada Eggon

There is a strong church under the EKAS MADA HILLS. There are areas yet to be evangelized.

Ibaji / Igala

These adjoin each other. The missionaries and pastors gave evidence of some 300 churches among the Igala and a strong work in Ibaji. Brethren Mission (CMML and Q.I.M).

Chawai

They are being evangelized with the help of their Katab and Kaje neighbors.

Jaba

There are a number of large churches and many towns are 50% Christia

Jukan

There are at least 15,000 believers - a good percentage.

Kamantan

They are being evangelized by their Kaje and Ijulu neighbors.

Lungu

A part of Jaba or Katab.

Mbula

The Lutheran Numan leaders spoke of strong churches among them.

Some that are unevangelized or partically evangelized but show evidence of being Islamized are the KAREKARE, GUNGAWA, DIBO (NUPE), NGIZIMI, MANDARA.

Summary of Strategic Methods of Evangelism

From Part One, Target Groups, I have selected a number of methods suggested there as they referred to the various groups, and presented them in summary form together with page numbers where they are found. What is applicable to one group may also be appropriate for another.

1. The use of Christian teachers as agents. During recent years there has been an explosion of school building programs throughout the northern states. This has called for a large increase in the teaching force. It is not unusual to find a Christian teacher in the midst of an almost total non-Christian community, he and his family being the only witness there. This is also true of agricultural assistants, nurses and dispensary attendants, etc. Such people could well serve as a base for further opening of the community. Opportunities like this will be multiplied during the next few years due to U.P.E. program. Pages 7 and 40.

2. In several places it has been noted that more than one denomination is involved in an area, and that there is need for them to work together. The work of evangelizing an area is not a competition. Converts do not "belong to us." They belong to God ultimately and we are His servants to bring them to Him. Therefore every effort should be made to sit down together and plan for the evangelization of an area. Page 8.

3. Homogenous unit churches will often help non-Christians to understand the gospel more quickly. The reason is that they feel more comfortable with their own people. This is not isolationism, but it is to help the unsaved to come to Christ without crossing unnecessary cultural barriers. Page 9.

4. Use of a team for service and evangelism. Demonstrated among the Busawa and the Mandara Mountain peoples. Page 12.

5. A mass effort by evangelists and pastors to plant churches as among the Maguzawa Hausa people. This has the tremendous advantage of a great impact in a short time. Where there is a ripened harvest it could result in many new converts and many new churches being started. Page 18.

6. Use of Community Development program as a base for training evangelists for church planting. Simple instruction and demonstration in use of improved seeds, fertilizers, insecticides and compost could give an evangelist tools for opening a new area. Poultry and rabbit husbandry together with care of fruit trees would give him additional income also. Certain already established stations could well be utilized as bases for such help. Page 17.

7. Volunteer evangelists go for three year period to plant churches in a new area to supplement what is already being done. Such a task force encourages the few who have been struggling alone. Page 17.

8. Gospel teams patterned after those of New Life for All should be used to supplement already established work. In this way when the workers leave after one or two months, the nearby church can continue to follow up the new converts. Page 20.

9. Bible School students often help pastors with new congregations during part of their holiday time. The young student gains experience and the pastor is able to open a new area which encourages the believers. The district churches should plan well in advance together with the students and principal of the school so that they will receive credit for their work. Pages 23 and 40.

10. A strong church among a people may often reach over to a nearby tribe and supply evangelists and pastors. In the opening of a work such workers will be the evangelists and church planters. As the church grows and is established they should be careful to make room for local people to become leaders as well. Page 35.

PART II

COMMENTS ON CULTURE

9

The Meaning of Culture

We are not just talking about traditional dancing, the vernacular language or the kind of food a certain group may eat. It goes beyond this to the total life style of a group. It may be described as a complete and detailed plan that embraces all aspects and needs of human life. But it is also the basic philosophy of a society which gives meaning to the outward manifestations. The basic religious concept of a society is not only a part of culture but the very heart of it (KATO, IFE 1975).

Since this is true, the introduction of the gospel will bring about changes in the life style of a group. But to change a part of a culture does not mean we need to throw out the whole thing. Here we need the wisdom and guidance of the Holy Spirit and caution should be exercised. The following comments gleaned from lectures by Dr. Donald R. Jacobs given at the Christian Education Strategy Conference sponsored by A.E.A.M. in Nairobi, January 1973, may help us to a right perspective.

Professor Mbiti makes the point that African cultures are incurably religious. Actually it is not possible for us to speak of a godless culture. And then going a step further, we may say that Jesus Christ both fulfills and judges the cultures of the people who believe on Him. He fulfills by enhancing and strengthening those parts of culture which are valuable and right. Family and clan ties are strong in Africa. Christ wants to fulfill these by bringing the family into the family of God. On the other hand, Jesus Christ judges the wrong in every culture and requires that it change.

People relate to each other in a culture by using symbols such as language, dress, certain habits and ways of living and earning a living. In order for communication to occur, the meanings given to these various symbols should be about the same. When someone changes these commonalities, then he is out of communication with the rest of the culture. This is important at the point of introducing the gospel to a culture. How much should these symbols change, if at all?

The Christian faith is not an addition to a person's culture, nor is it a culture of its own. The Christian faith is the person of Jesus Christ at work in the hearts of men and women in *their cultural setting*. Jesus Himself entered human experience and culture. He used our symbols of communication so that we could understand what He had to say. We must learn to communicate the gospel to a people using the symbols which they understand. When we insist on many changes, our message will appear foreign to them. Thi means then that Jesus does not call His people to remove themselves from their culture and tradition but promises them the wisdom and the power to live His life within their cultures. We do not ask people to turn their back upon their culture.

10

The Nature of Culture

Let us describe it in terms of four circles. Every person has
these four patterns within his life that make up his kind of
culture. A group of people with similar patterns are a cultural
group.

a. We begin with the inner core or PHILOSOPHY. The
    question here is: What is REAL? People who be-
    lieve that witchcraft and sorcery cause their prob-
    lems *attribute the cause of everything in the realm
    of the spiritual*. Therefore, they see no value in
    medicines or innoculations for the prevention of
    disease. This kind of thinking results in many
    outward practices. Farming is not begun until the
    gods are propiated and memorial feasts are held for
    the ancestors to insure their blessings. Change
    at the heart level is most difficult, but only when
    the heart is changed is there real conversion. Christ
    must be enthroned, then the outward manifestations
    will change easily as required.

    It is not uncommon for people to say they are Chris-
    tians and to think they actually are because they have
    taken on a certain manner of living such as church atten-
    dance and hymn singing. In reality changes in outward

form may be made without a heart change and usually
such people revert to their former ways of living.
In evangelism we are seeking to change the heart
by enthroning the Lord Jesus Christ which affects
all of a person's life style.

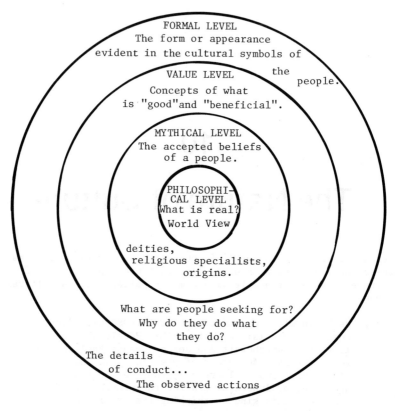

FORMAL LEVEL
The form or appearance
evident in the cultural symbols of the people.

VALUE LEVEL
Concepts of what
is "good"and "beneficial".

MYTHICAL LEVEL
The accepted beliefs
of a people.

PHILOSOPHICAL LEVEL
What is real?
World View

deities,
religious specialists,
origins.

What are people seeking for?
Why do they do what
they do?

The details
of conduct...
The observed actions

Table 1. The Four Levels of Culture

b. THE MYTHICAL LEVEL. This is the area of beliefs.
    There is a universal God concept, the creator and
    god of blessing. There are gods that bring trouble
    and the spirits of ancestors may even threaten them.
    Then there are the priests who seek to control the
    situations and interpret the messages from the spirit
    world. It is essential that the living be in contact
    with the dead. Dreams and visions need to be inter-
    preted. The core of the culture determines the set of

beliefs at this level. In contrast with this
Christians base their beliefs upon the Word of
God and that what it says is true. It has the word
of eternal life. It explains the beginning and the
end. It tells how man can be redeemed and become
a part of God's family. The believer must now
examine his traditional beliefs in the light of
the Bible. This is where the pastor or evangelist
needs to carefully interpret the Word of God in
terms of the culture.

c. AT THE VALUE LEVEL. What is important to people?
What is "good" for them? Dr. Kato expressed it this
way: "Every society has something it considers important, others more important and still a few others,
most important. For example, in an average African
society it is *important* to get married; *more important* to get married and have children; and *most important* to get married and have many children, but
most especially have male children."

Group solidarity is a high-ranking value in African
society. Jacobs feels it is the primary drive when
thought of in terms of family, clan or tribe. And
a corollary to this is the blessing of the group
for without it his very existence is threatened.
He gains status as he increases the group of people
who are indebted to him in some way. Jacobs also
lists a number of values that result from these
such as:
- It is important that you reproduce.
- You will defend the group against an intruder.
- You become a peacemaker when the group is
  threatened internally.
- It is important to have many people depending on you.
- You must strengthen the group. Help your nephew
  with school fees. (By so doing of course he and
  his father are indebted to you) (Jacobs 1973:34).

Another important value is that of fertility and
health. It is included above. Every group has a
god of fertility and rites that are performed annually for this purpose. Perhaps here we find a basic
reason for the practice of polygamy. In a part of
the world where up to 80% of the children died before age two years, fertility was extremely important to the family. What does the Word of God have
to say about these values? The importance of the
family is strengthened by the accounts of Noah,
Abraham, Jacob and the other patriarchs. Jesus and

His disciples later emphasized the need for household conversion. But the Bible goes beyond this to
the family of God universal, thus giving the family
a deeper meaning and even greater solidarity. Every
life is worth more than the wealth of the world put
together. New values will come in to replace the old
ones as a higher view of life is received. We must
interpret these values for them from the Word of God.

d. AT THE FORMAL LEVEL. "The layers of culture may
    also be compared to the different parts of an egg,
    the yolk, the white and the shell. The inside con-
    tent may be rotten, and yet the outward shell still
    gives the impression of a good egg. On the other
    hand a good egg may be tainted with some dirt on
    the shell and that is external" (Kato 1975).

    This is the level of observation, the detailed
    conduct of a people. Sometimes this is all that
    we understand of a culture because we haven't
    asked why do they do these things. Change is made
    most easily at this level.

    Dr. Jacobs summarizes: "The formal level is that
    level of culture in which the values and the philoso-
    phy are translated into forms. For instance, the
    idea that your existence is tied in with the group's
    existence is a philosophical assumption...Therefore
    you value the group above the individual. And from
    the value is produced the forms. Circumcision is
    a form. But it is a form of what? What is the
    value? What is this value built upon? So you go
    back to philosophy" (Jacobs 1973:34).

    This report points out a number of commonalities of
    culture among the various groups studied. They
    are displayed on the chart Appendix B. The purpose
    of this is to see the broad similarities upon which
    we may base a strategy for evangelizing these target
    groups. Further on we shall see how these can be
    used to smooth the approach to these peoples'
    minds. It is our responsibility as we invite people
    to become followers of Jesus Christ that we do not
    unnecessarily hinder them by erecting cultural bar-
    riers that God never intended.

    Some of the more important similarities at the
    formal level are the blood and grain sacrifices
    that are always accompanied with beer. There are the
    priests who act as mediators between the people and

the gods and spirits. Every group has its set of
tabus which must not be broken. Dreams and appear-
ances influence people very strongly. Medicines,
amulets, charms, fetishes are used by everyone to
protect and ward off evil. Then there are the rituals
to mark the passing from one stage of life to another--
birth, childhood, puberty, marriage, death, and the
wake following death.

The gospel messenger needs to carefully consider
the new forms that he introduces. What songs and
tunes should he use? How should he approach God
in prayer? Standing, sitting, kneeling, prone?
Is a pulpit appropriate when teaching the word?
Should people sit on mats, skins or chairs? This
is culture at the formal level. The people should
not feel uncomfortable with the forms you introduce.
Some forms will need to be changed. What substitu-
tions can be made? Youth camps may take the place
of initiation rituals.

Baptism symbolizes entry into the family of God.
Believers partake of the Lord's supper, symbolizing
the blood and the body of the Lord in remembrance
of Him. This takes the place of sacrifice which
Christ made once and for all. The relationship of
forms can thus be shown so that the transitions are
made more easily and are better understood in the
context of their experience.

11

The Impact of the Word of God on Culture

"Because no prophecy was ever made by an act of human will, but men moved by the Holy Spirit spoke from God" (11 Peter 1:21). The Bible came to us through the Hebrew and Greek cultures of the writers' times. These cultures were used as vehicles for conveying God's truth. God was not afraid to put His truth into the thought forms of an earthly culture for that was the only way He could get His message to men. But He controlled the writers and their language so that what they wrote was truly God's own thoughts and words...(Excerpted from B. Kato IFE lecture).

Therefore the content of the Bible is inspired and it cannot be changed. Cultures have deteriorated and changed many times across the world. God's Word is constant and therefore judges culture. God's Word is the norm and where the culture varies from that norm it is wrong and stands to be corrected. But the way in which we express the gospel and communicate its message may take different forms. Here we need to be sensitive to the cultural forms and values.

What are the social patterns in the new culture? To whom should we first speak? If a young person is addressing an elder, how should he begin? When should he speak? Every culture defines these situations. How does one make his message relevant as to content and form of communication? Should he preach a homiletical message, tell a story, use a proverb or a parable? How do people usually learn something new? Should the message be dramatized or demonstrated in some way? Is it proper to stand up or sit down? All these and many other questions related to culture should be given thought and preparation made accordingly. These are adjustable cultural forms through which the unchanging message of the Word of God will flow to the people. If the forms are right and do not make the people uncomfortable it will be much easier for them to grasp the truth. Often we have raised barriers for people to cross. The offense of the cross is one thing. The offense of violating cultural forms unnecessarily is another matter, and where possible should be avoided.

12

Cultural Commonalities and Church Planting

In the consideration of a strategy for cross cultural evangelism we must give thought to those cultural values and forms which are common to most groups in central Nigeria. The question is how can we best utilize these as vehicles for making the gospel relevent to the group we want to reach. We Christians have aquired new forms and values from our long association with believers and from the word of God. It is possible for us to expect others to have the same understanding or at best to wonder why they don't understand us. These fall into three general areas of Social, Occupational and Religious.

A. SOCIAL COMMONALITIES

1. *Family Ties*. We have already mentioned group or family solidarity as being the primary drive culturally speaking. The worst offense of a child is to disobey his parents or to initiate some new action without consulting them. Should evangelism then begin with children unless the "fathers" have understood the implications of it and have agreed for their children to become Christian? The elders usually understand that the "new way" is going to cut across their traditional beliefs. They view it as breaking up their normal patterns of living. And we can't deny this. But we could help them to see that by following Jesus they are brought into a much greater family--the family of God. God sent His Son to prepare us to enter His home and become His children. John 14.

2. *Marriage.* Polygamy stands at the top of the list of cultural practices that hinder people becoming Christian. We need to affirm the truth that God's ideal is one man and one woman joined in marriage. The two become one flesh. Genesis 2. Again in Genesis 6 we find Noah and his three sons and each one with one wife. They were the only righteous ones in that day. Jesus also emphasized this truth. Mark 10:6-9. But having said this we also find many men in the Old Testament who had more than one wife; Abraham, Jacob, David, Solomon to mention a few. God did not reject them because of this. Polygamy brought them many problems. They were still His children and His chosen ones. It is still true today that one may become a child of God together with his wives. According to their culture they did what they considered to be right. This is not just an African problem, it is a real problem all over the world. We must help people like this to cross this cultural barrier and make them understand that they are no less children of God because of it and have full right to enter His kingdom. It may be that God will open the way for them to change this situation later without hurting any of the people involved.

3. *Ancestors.* A part of the total family are those who have already died. In the animistic belief their spirits may return to help them and their blessing is invoked through feasts and sacrifices. To do anything contrary to the way of the ancestors violates the group's customs and will bring trouble upon them. How do we handle this keystone in African culture? Do not belittle their ancestors. Remember Abraham purchased a burial ground for his family and Joseph requested that his bones be carried up out of Egypt and buried with his fathers. Genesis 23:17-20; 50:5 and 25. It is normal to show respect for our forefathers. But there is more than this. Life goes on after the grave, and we must be prepared for it. Psalm 73:21-26. Job 19:25-27. In 1 Cor. 13:12 we read that we are still in the dark about many things but fuller light is ahead. There is even a time of resurrection when we will be joined with those who have passed on in Christ. 1 Th.4:16,17 and 1 John 3:2. Rather than tell people that they are completely wrong, show them that even God's ancient people held similar beliefs but that now there is more light. This subject of ancestors should also be linked with the matter of rebirth of a soul after death.

4. *Family Clan Structures and Village Tribal Heirarchy.* It is important that the evangelist begins with the right people, whether it is helping them with literacy, medicine or sharing the gospel. In the eyes of the community their important people should come first. In one community it was found wise to first teach the chief and his wife to read so that he would not lose status by others getting this valuable tool ahead of him. It may not be

meaningful in terms of the community thinking to help a blind
person or a leper in the beginning. They are outcasts anyway.
In one Muslim city the emir suffered greatly with an eye infection
that medicine did not help. Christians offered to pray for him
and he was healed. The result is an open door.

5. *Desire for Education.* I think it is safe to say that
Universal Primary Education scheme for Nigeria will provide new
motivation for the youth and young adults to learn to read. In
some of these groups it is still unpopular for children to go to
school. But that cannot continue for long. People must come to
terms with modern life and reality. If this is so we should be
ready to meet this felt need with an adequate literacy program.
It may be necessary to offer some English. The Catholics have
done this for many years. This should not be seen as "bribing"
a person to become a Christian. But it does lower his resistance
to it and he is able to listen and consider it. Simple primers
are already available in Hausa that provide relevant reading
materials on such subjects as family care, hygiene, farming and
gardening.

B. *OCCUPATIONAL CULTURAL COMMONALITIES*

These groups are 100% agricultural and with some fishing and
hunting according to the country where they live. Their usual
crafts have to do with the articles which they need to make a
living and build their houses. Such artisans are blacksmiths,
woodcarvers, weavers, builders, thatchers, potters, plus some
specialties such as making of musical instruments.

For a Maguzawa man to be caught without grain even after two
or three years of drought would be humiliating. Status is often
determined by the size of farm one has or more importantly by the
number of bundles of grain he puts up. The evangelist who has no
interest in farming will be considered lazy and worthless and not
really a man. No amount of excuses will justify him. He should
not only be a farmer but he should be a *better farmer* than they
are. Here is where Community Development and Faith and Farm
type of projects can be of immense value. Better seeds, fertilizer
and insecticides will improve his yield with less work. But he
should not seek to be number one in the town. It is better if he
can build up the person who is traditionally the best farmer in
the group. This will further increase the local man's stature and
win an influential friend for the evangelist. This may also be
applied to animal husbandry, poultry raising and fruit trees.
In one place domestic bee keeping and production of honey has
raised the people's standard of living.

C. FELT NEEDS

The lack of medical care in the remote areas is a common problem.
Most have no knowledge of simple hygiene and many die because they
do not know how to care for themselves. They still attribute
disease and epidemics to spirit influence.

Literacy is another felt need for many. Although the mother
tongue may not have been reduced to writing, there are excellent
literacy courses in Hausa.

The team approach that includes evangelist, nurse, literacy
worker, and agriculturalist is proving effective.
The team spends several days in a town including the market day
and ministers to a variety of needs during the day. At night they
sing, testify, dramatize and preach the gospel. This is useful
for awakening a sense of need within people and gaining entrance
to their lives.

D. RELIGIOUS

1. *High God.* In every group there is the belief in a High
God. He created the world and living things. He is responsible
for life today. Often prayer is offered to him for fertility and
fruitful farms. In some cases, he is the Sun which is the giver
of light and life. But they have little to do with this high
god. Instead there are a number of lesser gods with whom they
deal in daily life. One is reminded of Romans 1:21-23. What
does the Christian evangelist have to say in this situation?

The remnant of truth is there. It hasn't been lost entirely,
but it is distorted. We must explain from the Bible who God
really is and what His relationship is to man. Why is He so distant
and not understood? We must be careful when using the Hausa word
"Allah", lest they think our God is the same. Through the Bible
accounts of God's dealing with men in the Old Testament, we can
present a clear picture of our God who loves men. See the lesson
set, Appendix C.

2. *Rebirth.* When a baby is born soon after the death of an
old man or the mother dies in childbirth, the soul of the deceased
may have entered the baby and thus is reborn. Every group has
a tabu on certain animals because it is in some way linked with
people. There is a desire for continuity. This life cannot be
all there is. But what is in the next life? No one really knows
although the priests are expected to interpret these matters for
the living.

What does this have to do with our message of being "born again"? This is the true rebirth--the new life that never ends. First find out as much as you can about their particular beliefs in rebirth. Then you can point out that true rebirth is that of the spirit of man while he is still living and prepares one for eternal life. It is God who does this for man when he believes in His Son, Jesus Christ. The reborn one has a NEW LIFE; a new understanding of spiritual things; God's Spirit living in him to give power and wisdom, eternal life and sins forgiven and peace with God forever.

3. *Death.* It is a common belief that death is caused by sorcery (maita) or witchcraft eating another's spirit. So there is a witch hunt to find out who it was. Powerful medicine is concocted to counteract this.

God's word teaches that death came into the world because of sin and Satan (Genesis 3). The wages of sin is death (Romans 6:23). All the illness, evil, disease, murder and assault is from Satan. But some day death will end in God's Kingdom. Today Jesus Christ takes the stinger out of the scorpion's tail (1 Cor. 15:55-57). But every man will die physically (Romans 5:12). More important is the judgment that follows death unless you hide in Jesus Christ (John 5:24; Hebrews 9:27).

4. *Power Encounter.* The evangelist should be alert to and aware of any opportunity to serve the community in Jesus' Name. He should be willing to exercise faith even in desperate situations. Does our God have real power and loving concern? A demonstration is often necessary to convince the people. This we may call a Power Encounter. Elijah had such an encounter with Ahab and Jezebel. A member of a gospel team N.L.F.A. entered a village and preached. A mother thrust a child with a high fever into his arms and said, "Man of God, heal my baby." He was not prepared for this. He prayed in desperation. God answered. The church began that day.

5. *Priests.* Every people has a system of priests who act as mediators and interpreters in worship rituals. Sometimes it is the family head as Abraham did for his family. It may be the clan appoints a person or a group for this. The priest must know the will of the gods and the ancestors. He prays. He offers appropriate sacrifices and discovers who is to blame for a calamity. He may invoke a curse on another's enemy or prepare the medicine and fetishes to protect one or harm another. Since he is zealous of his position and authority, he resents anyone who threatens him such as the evangelist. He is the key man in the group.

God instituted priests as soon as man sinned. Adam offered a sacrifice. Noah and Abraham were priests. Melchizedek was priest of the Most High God. Later God chose Levites to be priests for Israel. Aaron was the high priest and stood between God and men. He was holy and clean and spoke God's message and did God's work (Heb. 10:19-25). Other kinds of priests are not needed.

This brief introduction to the problems associated with culture as well as the many points of contact it gives the evangelist should encourage each of us to investigate carefully the culture in which we are working. May it also help us to be sensitive to the way other people live.

PART III

STRATEGY:
STEPS FOR EVANGELISM AND CHURCH PLANTING

13

Strategy Planning

A strategy is really a plan for doing the work. Every part of
this report is an aid to help us to plan a strategy. The data
form supplies many items of information. The cultural form
shows the many commonalities of culture in these groups and
the emphasis of each in the culture. The target groups are
further described and cultural characteristics are shown to be
useful in our approach to the group. I want to describe two
planning aids so that we can think clearly about strategy.

1. PLANNING STRATEGIES FOR EVANGELISM - a workbook by Edward R.
Dayton
Available at M.A.R.C. (Mission Advanced Research & Communication
Center). An abridged form was supplied to the workshop on
Unreached People at the IFE National Congress on Evangelism and
may still be available at S.I.M., Jos. "This workbook is designed
to help you think about how to discover your role in God's
strategy for evangelism. It is meant to be used by Pastors and
Christian leaders trying to think through ways to evangelize their
locality." This workbook will enable you to sit down with your
people and find the answers to the situation of the group that
you want to evangelize. This is the first step.

2. *THE STRATEGY WHEEL*

This is a device (shown below) to help you divide up the various elements of a strategy and get them into some kind of order in your mind. Here again a group of leaders should work together. Note that every section or category is really dependent upon every other category. No category is independent or stands alone. They all interact with each other to produce the elements of the strategy. Here is how it works.

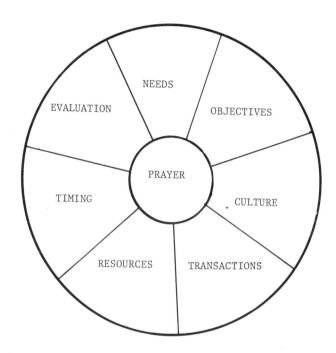

Table 2. The *STRATEGY WHEEL* makes planning easier and more accurate.

1. Needs. List the needs of the group to be evangelized. Write on the blackboard or a sheet of paper all that you can think of. Know God - Bible - Medical help - Literacy - Wells for Drinking Water - Clinic, etc.

2. *Objectives*. What do you want to accomplish. Try to be specific in terms of number of churches, towns, felt needs, etc. List these on another paper.

3. *Culture*. How does their culture affect your objectives? What particular values and forms must you take notice of?

4. *Transactions*. What steps must you take to accomplish your objectives? Objectives depended upon the needs you found. The transactions depend upon what your objectives are as seen through the culture. The culture is like colored glasses that help you to view everything in the right light.

5. *Resources*. Who is going to do the work? Who will carry out your transactions? How many evangelists, gospel teams, missionaries will you need? How much money? What equipment will be required? Literature, films, literacy primers, cassettes and players, posters, gramophones and records, housing, transport, etc.

6. *Timing*. How long will each step take? Preparations before entering the field? Initial contacts? When will each town be entered?

7. *Evaluation*. Although this is placed last it must not wait until the end. One must continually check on the progress he is making. It may be necessary to make a change in plans after two months. Or a new idea is brought in. Evaluation keeps us up to date and helps us to improve our work. If the goals have been stated in measurable terms then we can measure progress easily.

The above is the first step in planning--laying everything out where you can see it. Remember that your great objective is to evangelize this group and plant the church of Jesus Christ among them so that it will become a responsible reproducing church and continue to grow throughout the group.

Once you have determined your objectives and decided upon available resources then it is a matter of working out the series of transactions or steps that will bring you to the fulfillment of your objectives. This is really the critical part of the strategy. See now the diagram *AN EVANGELISM AND CHURCH PLANT-ING MODEL (Page 69)*.

14

An Evangelism and Church Planting Model

Jesus commanded His disciples to "MAKE DISCIPLES." This He said was to be accomplished by "going, baptizing, teaching." Matt. 28:18-20. In this model each phase has three steps. Each is a distinct step in the total process of discipling a group. The steps interlock with each other and often overlap so that lines are not always clearly defined, but each step has its own emphasis and reason for being included. In some groups Step One may already be completed and the work well advanced in Step Two. But every group should find itself somewhere on the outer circle and perhaps at several points depending upon progress made.

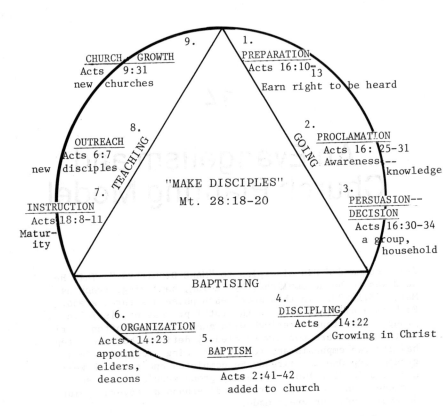

Table 3. Evangelism and Church Planting Model

    Take now your sheet of transactions and put it beside this
model with its nine steps on the outer circle. You may put all
of your transactions under these steps. Check your steps
against those on this page. There may be some that you didn't

think of. No list is ever complete. You will be adding others
as you plan and begin to do the actual work of church planting.

STEPS	*TRANSACTIONS*

1. *Preparation*
   Earn the right to be
   heard

   1-6 months

   a. Choice of location
   b. Building people's confidence in you
   c. Observing responses of the people
   d. Making friends
   e. Meeting a felt need

2. *Proclamation*
   But no response
   required yet

   3-12 months

   a,b may occur in 1.

   a. Announcement of purpose
   b. Identify yourself
   c. Make aware of your message
   d. Add knowledge through content of
                               message
   e. Use of Bible stories
   f. Power encounter as God leads

3. *Persuasion/Decision*
   A group, household

   a. A number show desire to become
                               Christian
   b. Some ask questions
   c. Ask them to consider Jesus Christ
   d. Provide opportunity for decision
                           to follow Jesus
   e. Reinforce decision with discussion,
      answer questions, explanation of
                           God's family

4. *Discipling*
   Growing in Christ

   3-6 months

   a. Worship and prayer
   b. Fellowship
   c. Teaching
   d. Witness
   e. Stewardship of life and possessions

5. *Baptism*
   Added to the church

   a. Baptismal service
   b. Responsible members
   c. Disciple others

6. *Organization*

   Appoint elders, deacons each
   with a function in the local church

7. *Instruction*
   Maturity in Christ

   a. All things I have told you
      Matt. 28:20, Col. 2:6,7
   b. Lay leadership training
   c. Courses in T.E.C. / weekend a month /
      course ten days

8. *Outreach*   a. Local witness
   New disciples   b. Village visitation
                          c. Classes in villages

9. *Church Growth*   a. Local church growth
   New churches   b. New churches in villages
                          c. Missionary outreach

EXPLANATION OF EVANGELISM/CHURCH PLANTING MODEL

1. *Preparation*. As pointed out under the section on Culture
it is most important that we begin with the right people and in
the right manner. Natural leaders of the group should be respected
and consulted. Their friendship and confidence cultivated. During
this time more exact information may be obtained on the local
customs and patterns and the data form may be refined and details
filled in. Felt needs should be assessed and perhaps a simple
beginning can be made toward meeting one of them. The whole
purpose of this step is to lay the groundwork and the foundation
for the PROCLAMATION STEP in such a way that people will be ready
and eager to listen to your message. One "earns the right to be
heard" by showing a genuine love and concern for people.

2. *Proclamation*. Since our objective is not only to evangelize
but also to make disciples and plant churches, the proclamation of
the gospel should be structured in such a way that this worthy
objective may be attained as quickly as possible. The oft used
method of itinerating and "preaching the gospel" without any thought
for what the preceding message said or what is to follow later does
not usually build up a knowledge of God and His purpose for man in
the minds of people.

A number of church planters have used a planned teaching program
directed at a related group of people with real success. Grimley
reports on the Sevav plan introduced among the Tiv in 1962 by
Rubingh and Baker of the Christian Reformed Church (SUM/CRC). This
was based on the fact that each person is a member of a tribe, clan
and extended family. The core of the plan called for a systematic
weekly witness over a period of several months. During this time
a series of lessons in form of Bible stories were taught to a
clan group. At the close a three-day conference was held and
people were invited to decide for Christ. They reported that in
the first three places approximately 20 responded in each clan.
This represented about 20% of the clan adults. These then continued in a discipleship training class. (GRIMLEY 1966:216-219).

The heart of this strategy is the series of lessons in Bible
story form. The people learn more easily through stories. The
stories contain truths about God, man and sin and God's way of

saving man. By returning weekly over a period of months and
and speaking to very much the same group of people you develop
a group consciousness within them. They begin to discuss the
stories and truths among themselves and unconsciously draw con-
clusions about them. Since they are accustomed to making group
decisions about every important matter of life, it is only normal
that they would want to discuss God's way of salvation for them
and make a decision about it. The aim is to so prepare a core
group through the teaching and discussions that a group of responsible adults will make the decision together to follow Jesus
Christ. Such a plan has also been worked out to assist in the
evangelizing of the Fulani people.

I recommend that you study the Sevav Plan carefully as described
by Grimley. Another similar model was devised by A.C. Krass in
Ghana and is described by McGavran in "Understanding Church Growth,"
(1970:331-334). The Fulani model is fully described in the book
TAIMAKO GA FULANI (Hausa) and is available at Christian Bookstores
in Nigeria.

3. Persuasion - Decision. During the period of proclamation
you haven't asked for a decision. But you have been sowing the
idea in their minds that God's way is much better than theirs
and offers them much more. They also have begun to get some idea
about God and His love and purpose for man. Now comes the time
for drawing the net. The evangelist must be sensitive to the
Spirit's leading and not force decisions by undue efforts to per-
suade people. Usually one can tell by the kinds of questions that
people ask and the response to the discussions. Make it plain to
them that they are entering the family of God and there are certain responsibilities and ways of living in the family. This is
the time for repentance, "turning from idols to serve the living
God and to wait for His Son from heaven" (1 Th. 1:9,10).

4. Discipling. Preparation should have been made for this
well beforehand. The next few months are critical just as it is
for a newborn baby. They must be fed with the proper food. You
may want to consider using the New Life for All book, "Going on
in the New Life". The 12 lessons are ideal for the early discipling process. They are written simply and meant to help the
babes in Christ learn what their new life in Christ is all about.

In Acts 2:41-47 we see the first church meeting together for
worship and prayer, fellowship, and instruction in the apostles
doctrine. They recognized that God had a claim upon their lives
and their possessions. They shared their faith with others and
daily new believers were added to the church. These are the elements of discipling and the church leader will be careful to help
them grow in Christ in these ways.

5. *Baptism.* Jesus Christ commanded his disciples to be baptized. This should be an important goal in the discipling process. They now become responsible members of the local church and should be ready to disciple others as well.

6. *Organization.* In the New Testament elders and deacons were appointed to minister to the people. Acts 6:1-6; 14:23; 1 Tim. 3.

7. *Instruction.* As Christ commanded, "teaching them to observe all things that I have commanded you," we need to faithfully instruct the believers. "Feed my sheep" Jesus told Peter. The Holy Spirit gives gifts to men so that they may minister to the Body. Ephesians 4:7-17. These men need training in the word. The T.E.E. program is being used very successfully in many places. Programmed Instruction manuals are available. In some cases where illiteracy is a problem cassette tapes are being used for the instruction input. Another method is to set up a short course of two weeks at intervals of three months for the purpose of giving leadership training. The Anglicans at Wusasa Zaria regularly conduct such leadership training courses with good results.

A manual, 24 stories, is available in English and Hausa. It was originally written to provide help to untrained leaders of village churches in the conduct of worship and in sharing the Good News. Paul wrote "And we proclaim Him admonishing every man and teaching every man with all wisdom, that we may present every man complete in Christ" (Colossians 1:28).

8. *Outreach.* From the very outset the early church began to grow rapidly due to the daily witness of its numbers. Acts 2:47; 8:1-3. Every believer is a witness. Acts 1:8. Sharing the good news is the normal way of life for Christians. A vital part of instruction will be to help them know how to do this. Other villages around them need to hear and are their responsibility. New classes need to be begun so that daughter churches may be opened soon. This will result in the last step.

9. *Church Growth.* As it is normal for every living thing to grow, so it is normal for the church, the Body of Christ, to grow. When each member is functioning in the body according to its gift and ability then the body will grow. In the New Testament we hear that the church was multiplied throughout Judea, Galilee and Samaria. Acts 9:31. That is, local churches sprang up everywhere. In addition every local church should be involved in outreach beyond its own people.

Now we have come full circle. These nine steps lead us through the full cycle of evangelism and church planting. It will take longer in some areas than in others. But where careful, prayerful planning has preceded the effort and applications of church growth strategy have been used, there will be a bountiful harvest. Many will enter the family of God and His Name will be praised.

PAUL'S MODEL FOR CHURCH PLANTING AT PHILIPPI

Turn to Acts 16:10-40 and study carefully the following outline. Check it against the model we have just made and see how it compares.

STEPS	*CH. 16*	*DESCRIPTION*
1	v. 10	A conviction of God's direction
	v. 11	A forward move in that direction
	v. 12	Choice of right place to begin - 'the leading city'
	v. 13	Chose a possible responsive audience 'place of prayer'
2	v. 14,15	An influential person opened her heart and home
	v. 16	Continued to visit same place - further developed it
	v. 16	A power encounter with Satanic force
	v. 19-24	Persecution arises
	v. 25-34	Missionaries continue to use every opportunity.
3,5	v. 31-34	Household now believes and is baptized Note question asked
4	v.35-39	Not intimidated by officials, states his rights as a citizen
	v. 40	Visits, comforts, strengthens believers
6-9	Phil.1:1	Church growth; saints, leaders now in charge
	2:25;4:18	Epaphroditus. dedicated servant of the Lord
	4:10-16	Missionary concern, shared with Paul Helped in church planting in Thessalonica.

15

Use of the Media

The local church is the agent and the goal of evangelism. The people in the local church are the basic resource. But people work through various channels or media to communicate the message of the gospel. The right use of the various media will strengthen the message and speed up the whole process of evangelization. In order to do this the right "media-mix" is required. Each channel has an area in communication that it does best.

In his book, Cassette Ministry, Victor Sogaard presents us with a basic segmentation model for gospel communication (p.28). He then enlarges this to show the spiritual position of man on that model (p. 29). See next page.

This is very helpful because it enables us to plug in the various media at the place on the segmentation model where each is most effective. For a given program of evangelism/church planting one can decide which media he should use and therefore which media-mix will be most effedtive. Sogaard makes an important statement about evangelism on p. 116. "In evangelism the cassette ministry must be integrated with the general outreach of the church. In this way it will expand and strengthen that ministry." This can be said equally of any medium. The personal worker may multiply the effectiveness of his ministry with cassettes. But the cassettes will not be effective without that personal worker. We must never lose sight of this fact. What are some of the basic factors that relate to the media in our kind of program? Each group strategy will be different due to availability of resources and other circumstances. Nevertheless there are a number of basic factors common to any program.

We will discuss four channels in the media-mix and suggest ways that they can be integrated with the outreach of the local church. But first note the place of decision on the scale below. It is preceded by a lot of communication which is termed sowing. One of the mistakes the over zealous evangelist and radio preacher often make is that of always calling for a decision. In the first place, the kind of message given during the sowing period differs greatly from that used during reaping time. In this strategy a lesson series of Bible stories has been suggested and outlined. These are to be plugged in on the scale from A to J. They will fulfill the intent of D,G. & J and make it possible for people to decide intelligently.

1. Radio. Radio is a fantastic tool for reaching masses of people. In the remote areas it is almost the only means of touch with the outside world. It is probably safe to assume that nearly every village has at least one radio receiver and very likely more than one.

There are Christian radio stations such as R.V.O.G. and E.L.W.A. In Nigeria radio stations are either State or Nationally controlled. We call these secular. Research and experience tell us that the Christian stations have mostly a Christian audience. Non-Christians, and most Christians, tune in to the secular station and keep it open all day. Today opportunities are opening on the State controlled stations for Christian programming. We need to investigate these openings and prepare the kind of program that will help our people. This is not to ignore the great usefulness of the Christian stations. They are regularly broadcasting good programs in Hausa, Fulani, Yoruba, Ibo, Nupe and other languages.

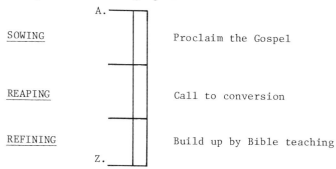

A.

SOWING — Proclaim the Gospel

REAPING — Call to conversion

REFINING — Build up by Bible teaching

Z.

Table 4. Every man can be represented on the scale from A. to Z., from the one who knows nothing about the gospel to the most mature.

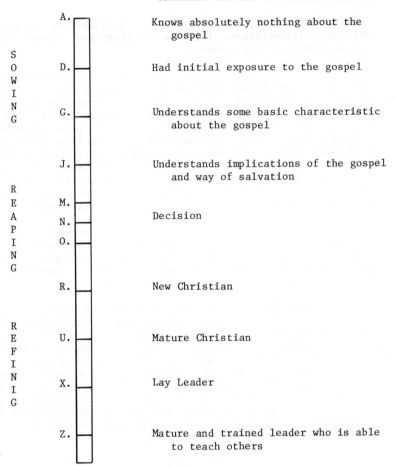

Table 5.   The Spiritual Position of Man on Segmentation
           Model (Sogaard)

Many minds especially among the Muslims are being opened to the
light. Research indicates that the awakening among the Fulani is
largely due to radio programs.

What then is the best use of radio in evangelism? What kind of
programming should be aired? Sogaard suggests these advantages of
radio:
   Radio can give knowledge and widen horizons
   - focuses attention on the teachings of Christ
   - raises aspirations for change
   - can help to change attitudes

- is believed, and in time will give a good understanding
  of Christian words, concepts and beliefs
- gets into closed homes such as of the elite and strong
  religionist.

For purposes of evangelism radio is best used as a SOWING medium.
Our programming therefore should be aimed at producing what radio
does best. A program in Hausa and Fulani using the Bible stories
in the series would integrate with the local church outreach. It
would reinforce the message of the evangelist and add credibility
to his words. It would bring increased understanding and hasten
the time for decision. In many villages the way would be cleared
before him prior to his coming thus lessening preparation time.
Therefore we plug radio into our scale from A to J or M. Again
it is very useful for Christians in order to build them up with
teaching: O to U.

2. Cassette. Most of us are familiar with this very excellent
communication medium but have we realized its potential for evangelism and church planting. It can be used by the Christian while
he is present or he can leave it with an interested person. Around
Maradi, Republique du Niger, today there are some 30 cassette
players in regular use on this loan basis. Cassettes are kept cir-
culating by a few keen Christians. New cassettes are being con-
stantly produced to satisfy the tremendous thirst for knowledge.
The audience are people who have been resistant to the gospel for
many years of gospel preaching. The cassette seems to act as a
third person and thus lowers the feeling of confrontation with the
evangelist even though he may be sitting right there. They are
used over and over again for the benefit of all the neighbors. It
must be integrated with the personal work of the believer at the
time of his regular visit. Used in this way it becomes an excellent medium to bring people to a decision for Christ.

When preparing the program it must be remembered that the
cassette is for sowing and not for harvesting. Sogaard suggests
that you don't just preach, but ask some questions. The listener
whould be engaged in the communication so that he is actively thinking about the subject. The message must be friendly and positive
(SOGAARD 1975:112-123).

Further down the segmentation scale we find that the cassette
is also very useful for teaching and training purposes. So we can
plug it in at A to M and again from O to Z. A very versatile
medium.

3. Literature. The vast majority of members (probably 95-98
percent) of the group we are considering are functionally illiterate.
With the advent of the U.P.E. this may begin to change rapidly. For
the present we need to think in terms of visualizing the gospel for
the non-reader. Some experience in this was gained in New Life for
All and may very well be applied to our target groups.

If we accept a set of Bible stories as the basis for the sowing ministry then a cartoon type picture could be produced for each story. It would have to be very simple with a single focus. They would be produced cheaply for mass distribution by those who are telling the story. On the back side a few lines emphasizing the teaching of the story or a verse of scripture would help any possible reader as well. Such a visual aid would further reinforce the message and be a reminder of it during his absence.

There is an abundance of graded literature available to the new Christian and for those going on to maturity. Besides primers in Hausa, there are some in other vernaculars as well as some of the gospels. Books for new readers, tracts, catechism type studies, baptismal class materials, Sunday School lessons and commentaries are available in Hausa. The T.E.E. program has produced several books of self-instruction programmed materials. These are excellent for lay leadership training.

4. *Film*. Films have now been used widely for evangelism and often the unsophisticated audience does not comprehend them. However, by turning the sound off, a good narrator can be used instead to convey the message in the language best understood. The filmstrip is really more adaptable than the cinema and the equipment is more easily obtained. The narrator can proceed at his own pace according to the audience level of comprehension. The Bible story filmstrips could be integrated with the same stories of the lesson set. I see this mainly as a part of the sowing ministry. However, a filmstrip or cinema on the crucifixion and resurrection may very well provide an opportunity for reaping if there has been sufficient sowing beforehand.

5. *Media Mix*. The strategy of the media by now is apparent. The message should be determined upon and then the media should be integrated to that message for maximum effect. This would require a united effort on the part of all who are concerned with these target groups. God has placed the tools in our hands. We need to lay our plans well for their best use.

See Appendix D for diagram of a suggested Media Strategy for Target Groups.

6. *Other Media*. The gramophone has been very useful in the past. Gospel Recordings has recorded gospel messages and songs in more than 400 Nigerian languages. These are available in form of records 78 RPM and 33 LP; as Cardtalks where one uses an ordinary pencil to play the "card record"; and cassettes. A complete listing of these is available at Gospel Recordings.

Posters are also useful to keep people reminded of the message. Scripture Gift Mission is willing to supply a wide variety of Scripture text posters in several main languages to careful distributors. New Life for All may have a supply on hand.

There are a large number of tracts available some of which are quite useful. Perhaps new ones should be written with these target groups in focus, keeping in mind the low literacy rate but also the newly emerging readers in the schools.

Drama is being used by the Basel Mission teams in their evening gatherings. The acting out of Bible stories and themes is very effective. Young people especially enjoy this and often are eager to take part. They thus have a meaningful avenue of service.

Songs are a medium of communication. New songs in the vernacular languages need to be composed and set to familiar tunes. In the total media needs there are challenges for many to take part and make a contribution.

Every effective channel needs to be brought into focus for reaching these target groups.

16

Resources

Needs have to be matched with resources. We have already seen the
tremendous needs of these thirty or more peoples in Central
Nigeria. Certain strategic methods have been suggested. But
what are our resources in terms of people and pastors, institutions
media and finances for the execution of the strategy in order to
accomplish our objectives.

GOD'S PEOPLE

God's people are the channel through which He has chosen to reach
out to others who are not yet "His sheep". A study of the accompanying tables and graphs reveals that there is a community of
evangelical believers numbering more than 1.5 million and 6,500
local churches where these people gather for weekly worship. Of
this number 200,000 are members and they are led by 5,000 men
trained in the Word of God to various degrees. Certainly God has
raised up a mighty testimony to His grace and faithfulness throughout the land. The question then is, how can they be mobilized
for the remaining task of evangelism and church planting?

It should be noted that, generally speaking, in the areas
adjoining the unevangelized peoples the church is the weakest.
This means that a special effort by the stronger churches in the
heart of central Nigeria (Plateau, Benue, Kaduna and Kwara States)
will have to be made. For them it will mean looking beyond their
borders, literally "lifting up their eyes" to the harvest fields.

The group of churches under the banner of TEKAS work in close fellowship with each other in Gongola, Plateau and Benue States. It would seem natural for them to consult together about increasing their outreach to the most needy places within these states where they are already committed. Although the burden of the work will fall upon them, they must bear in mind the existence of other groups as well, such as the Baptists, Assemblies of God, Anglicans and others who may want to have a part in an extended outreach. The need is for all who are directly concerned to come together to plan for the utilization of their resources in the best possible way.

During the six-year period 1967-73 TEKAS church attendance nearly tripled to more than one million while membership increased by two-thirds. Giving more than doubled during this brief span and local churches increased by 642 from 4,000.

The next largest group of churches is that of ECWA which works mainly in Kaduna, Plateau, Bauchi, Niger and Kwara States. The work of ECWA in Bauchi and Borno has a solid base but it is not large except in the Tangale Waja area. Perhaps these latter can offer help to their brethren in order to reach the seven groups who are within the area of their combined influence. Again in Minna division of Niger State ECWA finds itself with a struggling church among the Gbari Yamma and the Kamuku. This is an area where the Baptists are strong and it would be advantageous for these two groups to plan together.

In western Niger State, Kontagora division the work is largely being done by the U.M.C.A. churches. In order to reach the Kambari people and other groups they will need help.

The strong church area of southern Kaduna State with its thousands of believers is ideally suited to give help in any direction. The Maguzawa people are already the objective of ECWA, Baptist and Anglican workers, but only the fringes are being touched. The harvest is ripe, the laborers are few.

In Kwara State there is a large community of Yoruba believers divided among the Baptists, Anglicans, ECWA and others. Culturally they are ideally suited to reach out to the Igbirra people to the east. However the Busa people in the northern part of the state are more culturally related to the Hausa-speaking peoples and should look to them for help. As noted in the Busa section it is the Methodist church that has taken responsibility here but they are greatly in need of reinforcements.

The statistical tables show growing churches. A recent church growth workshop confirmed this trend. It seems fair then to assume that our people resources will continue to expand rapidly. This will provide us with a continuing larger base from which to launch the evangelism church planting program.

Two missionary organizations are associated with the churches.
The EKAS PLATEAU church has sent its missionaries into Borno Lake
Chad area as well as to the Gwoza district. The latter are making
a great contribution to church planting in the Mandara Mountains.
It is hoped that this kind of effort will be increased and that
other church groups will follow this plan of outreach.

The ECWA churches have sponsored the Evangelical Missionary
Society (EMS) and now have 125 couples ministering in many parts
of Nigeria and other countries. Some of the people in this report
among whom they are working are the Bassa, Afo, Gade, Gwandara,
Alago in Plateau State; Hausa Maguzawa, Kadara and Koro in Kaduna
State; Afawa, Warji and Miya, Zaranda Hill and Jarawa in Bauchi
State; the Kamuku and Gbari in Niger State. Missionaries of both
groups are supported by contributions from local churches. When
they have successfully planted a church, a pastor is called and t
move on to another field.

Finally, it is the pastors and church leaders who need to prayer
fully consider the task together with all who are involved in it
in any way. It has been my experience that the people are ready
to give themselves for spreading the gospel when their leaders
show them the way. They need teaching and encouragement.

INSTITUTIONS

More than 25 Bible Schools and seminaries are available for the
training of leaders for the churches and their organizations. Thes
range from 2-4 year vernacular schools, Bible Colleges which are
4-year post primary schools, to the degree granting seminary. Of
the latter there are two within central Nigeria. Theological
College of Nigeria (TEKAS) at Bukuru, Plateau State, and the Ig
Theological Seminary (ECWA) in Kwara State. Bible Colleges at
Ayu (EKAS MADA), Bukuru (TEKAS), Kagoro (ECWA), Kaduna-Kawo (Baptist) are supplying English speaking graduates who are especially
needed in the city churches. As U.P.E. progresses the need for
these increases.

However, it is the large number of vernacular schools scattered
throughout each of the major church groups that has prepared a
strong corps of men for the ministry. They are the backbone of the
work in the thousands of villages. Many of these have taken additional studies and have been ordained. Hausa will continue to be
the major language of the people for many years to come. Therefore these schools are greatly needed as we look forward to planting many new churches. This policy is also necessary in view of
the great task of discipling (already noted above) that is upon
the church. In some cases the numbers of trained church leaders
is already running far behind the numbers of churches. This means
that many of the believers are being neglected and may result in
some of them turning away.

The challenge of these unevangelized groups must be set before
the students in these schools. They need to be taught church
planting methods so that they will know ho to go about their work.
May God give us hundreds who will volunteer for this ministry in
the next five years.

NEW LIFE FOR ALL is an institution in central Nigeria. It has
undoubtedly accounted for much of the rapid church growth in the
last ten years. All the pastors agree that it has contributed
more than other factors to the unity among the churches. N.F.L.A.
taught the churches how to mobilize and evangelize. It gave them
the concept of gospel teams going into new areas. It taught the
believers how to pray for unsaved friends and neighbors. Through
the handbook studies they learned what the gospel meant and how
to share it with others.

As a para church organization, N.L.F.A. could probably do more
than any other group to help the churches mobilize for this effort.
They are on a number of State radio programs. They have produced
good evangelistic literature for different kinds of people. They
can help in the training of gospel team units. The interdenominational aspect of N.L.F.A. will be of great value in getting different church groups to work together for the evangelization of a
particular people.

MEDIA MINISTRIES

Two important Christian Radio stations have recording studios in
central Nigeria. The Jos studio of Radio Voice of the Gospel
(Lutheran) records programs in Hausa and Fulani for broadcasting
later from Ethiopia. ELWA has a recording studio in Jos (SIM) for
Hausa programs and another in Igbaja for Yoruba, Nupe and English.
ELWA's transmitter is located in Liberia. Both of these stations
have given excellent cooperation to the evangelism programs of
New Life for All.

In an effort such as is envisaged to reach these 30 groups,
radio is very important. Many people in a community will hear
the same message. It will break down barriers. It can especially
be useful when coordinated with tape recorded stories placed in
the villages. Here is a valuable resource tool but it will take
careful planning and good programming to make it effective.

LABARUN KIRISTA (News for Christians) is a paper produced
jointly by TEKAS and ECWA. The paper has great potential for
communicating news. Presently it comes out quarterly, and is
seldom up to date. The readership is not as wide as it could
be. Perhaps if it were reporting on a good evangelism program,
there would be an increased interest in it.

EVANGELICAL LITERATURE FELLOWSHIP OF NIGERIA (ELFON) has co-ordinated the publication of the revised Hausa Hymnal, Sunday School manuals, and most recently, literacy primers in Hausa. ELFON is a fine resource organization that has earned the respect of all groups in Nigeria. It could coordinate production of lit-erature thus eliminating overlapping and duplication. One of the suggestions made earlier is that 'photo papers' be prepared to illustrate the Bible stories. Since these would be the same for every group, they could be mass produced. Such a project would logically come under ELFON.

BOOKSHOPS operated by C.S.S., EKAS, CHALLENGE and BAPTIST are necessary agents to the publishing medium so that distribution can be effected quickly. It is another resource in a long chain whose links are joined together in a common task.

The media are resource schools to be used by people. They can help to make people more effective. When the various media are coordinated their effectivenss is multiplied. All of this means that careful planning must precede and accompany this evangelism and church planting work.

FUNDS

God's work done in God's way will never lack God's supply. "My God shall supply all your need according to His riches in glory in Christ Jesus " (Phil. 4:19). Time after time I have seen God's people respond to great challenges to evangelize. When they are convinced of the importance of the work they always give abundantly. The resources of over one million believers are at God's disposal. Prayer and faith will release these.

Resources need to be guarded carefully lest they are wasted. Lack of coordination and proper planning causes waste of time and money. A carefully planned budget therefore is essential. In the Strategy Wheel diagram this is brought to our attention. Look at all the steps to action that you want to take. How much will each step cost? Now is the time to cut out unnecessary steps and thus save money. After each item is accounted for, arrange in an orderly way and find the total.

Now you are ready to carry the need to your people to seek their help. People want to know what they are giving for. To them it is an investment. What is the purpose of this investment? How is it going to be carried out? Who will do it? What will be the results? As the one who presents it to them you must be able to assure them with good answers. Ask them to pray about it and then to give as the Lord directs.

Church organizations need to put this work on their annual budgets also. All of our denominations state that evangelism is the reason for their existence. Oftentimes they earmark very little for evangelism and the church suffers. Evangelism stirs the hearts of God's people to prayer, witness, Bible study and giving of time and money. Where there is no vision, the people perish. Not only do the unsaved perish, but the children of God dry up and become fruitless.

The resources of the world belong to God--the cattle, the gold, the oil, everything. He can do far above all that we ask or think. Eph. 3:20.

	Places of Worship	Ordained Ministers	Lay Leaders	Members	Attendants
Baptist 1974*	2,143	964		119,881	350,000
ECWA	1,400	400	1,000	57,330	250,000
TEKAS	4,642	351	3,275	116,972	1,111,925
UMCA 1972				10,260	
Totals	8,183	1,715	4,275	304,443	1,711,925

Table 6.   Statistics for Major Denominations

* Baptist figures are for all of Nigeria.   Majority are Yoruba
in southern Nigeria

Branches	Places of Worship	Ordained Ministers	Lay Leaders	Members	Attendants
Benue	232	31	113	9,259	94,104
Gabas	344	71	353	22,704	31,919
Kaduna	13	3	4	1,217	3,711
Lutheran	872	57	879	21,855	518,331
Mada	370	20	329	8,923	11,481
Muri	229	31	126	7,042	25,969
Plateau	1,116	65	1,117	26,778	153,270
Tiv NKST	1,466	73	314	19,194	273,140
Totals	4,642	351	3,275	116,972	1,111,925

Table 7.   TEKAS Branches 1973

EKAS BRANCHES	1957	1967	1973
Benue	1,431	9,789	9,259
Gabas	3,373	17,527	22,704
Kaduna			1,217
Lutheran	6,800	18,294	21,855
Mada	1,121	3,363	8,923
Muri	578	2,701	7,042
Plateau	3,792	11,298	26,778
Tiv NKST	3,201	11,829	19,194
Totals	20,296	74,801	116,972

Table 8.   TEKAS Churches Membership Growth

	1961	1972
Bauchi	399	1,220
Borno		410
Eastern		720
Gwari	1,571	7,800
Kano	355	2,300
Nupe	185	900
Sokoto	48	630
Tangale Waja	2,700	7,800
Yoruba Ilorin Kabba Southern	4,000	6,700 6,100 3,350
Zaria	5,000	13,000
Plateau		6,400
Totals	14,258	57,330

Table 9. ECWA Membership by Districts

APPENDICES

A.

Frontier Peoples Data

BENUE-PLATEAU STATE

1. Alago
2. Afo
3. Bassa
4. Gade
5. Gwandara

KWARA STATE

6. Busa
7. Igbirra

NORTH CENTRAL STATE

8. Hausa Maguzawa
9. Kadara
10. Koro (data sheet omitted)

NORTH EAST STATE

11. Afawa
12. Butawa
13. Warji
14. Miya

NORTH EAST STATE continued:

15. Jarawa
16. Zaranda Hill (Geji, Zul, Bolu, Pelu, Girma)
17. Babur Thali
18. Ngamo
19. Mandara Mtns. (Zhaladivha, Hidkala, Dghwede, Guduf, Glavda, Ngoshe, Sukur, Tur, Vemgo)
20. Fali
21. Verre
22. Mumuye
23. Daka
24. Jibu
25. Ndoro

NORTH WEST STATE

26. Kambari
27. Duka
28. Fakai
29. Gbari Yamma
30. Kamuku

TARGET GROUPS ALPHABETICALLY LISTED

Target Group	State	Map No.	Page of Text
Afawa	Bauchi	11	20
Afo	Plateau	2	6
Alago	Plateau	1	5
Babur Thali	Borno	17	24
Bassa	Plateau	3	7
Busa	Kwara	6	11
Butawa	Bauchi	12	20
Daka	Gongola	23	34
Duka	Niger	27	39
Fakai	Niger	28	39
Fali	Gongola	20	31
Gade	Plateau	4	8
Gbari Yamma	Niger	29	40
Gwandara	Plateau	5	9
Hausa Maguzawa	Kaduna	8	14
Igbirra	Kwara	7	12
Jarawa	Bauchi	15	21
Jibu	Gongola	24	35
Kadara	Kaduna	9	16
Kambari	Niger	26	37
Kamuku	Niger	30	40
Koro	Kaduna	10	16
Mandara Mountains	Gongola	19	27
Miya	Bauchi	14	19
Mumuye	Gongola	22	33
Ndoro	Gongola	25	36
Ngamo	Borno	18	25
Vere	Gongola	21	32
Warji	Bauchi	13	20
Zaranda Hills	Bauchi	16	22

EXPLANATION OF TERMS USED IN DATA SHEET APPENDIX A

ATTITUDE TOWARD GOSPEL: 0 = unknown   3 = indifferent
                             1 = opposed   4 = receptive
                             2 = resistant   5 = responsive
CRITERIA FOR PRIORITY: A people who are

#1 = 0-10% evangelized / Evangelist only among them /few believers
     / receptive or responsive
#2 = 10-50% evangelized / established church /a strong church nearby
#3 = 50% or more evangelized but resistant / 10-50% evangelized
     but a progressive, growing church

IDENTIFICATION

1 GROUP NAME: Alago   2 POPULATION: 350,000

3 STATE/DIVISION Plateau-Lafia   4 ADMINISTRATIVE CENTRE : Lafia

5 LOCATION: N - Mada; W - Afo; S-E - Tiv

6 DESCRIPTION: A Eth Ling   B Villages   C Agric.

     Muri Div., Awe, Daddare, Obi, Adogi, Lafia

7 ACCESSIBILITY: Easy, rail, river, road

8 COMMUNICATION MEDIA: Postal Radio

9 DYNAMICS OF UNIT: Growing, stable, resisting change

10 INTERMARRIAGE: Yes

11 PART OF LARGER UNIT, NAME: No   RELATIONSHIP:

12 POPULATION CENTRES / MARKET (M) / SCHOOL (S)
   Doma (M) Kean - Obi   Lafia   Rutu (M)
               (S)

13 FARM CROPS: Yam, maize, millet, beniseed

14 MEDICAL FACILITIES: Dispensary Doma

LANGUAGE / LITERACY

15 PRINCIPAL VERNACULAR: Alago 100%   16 TRADE LANGUAGE: Hausa   95 % USERS

17 LITERATE ADULTS: few 5%   18 CHANGE IN LITERACY RATE: +

19 PER CENT CHRISTIANS WHO ARE LITERATE: 10 %

20 WHAT DO PEOPLE READ: Bible, Gaskiya Books

21 ESTIMATED ALJEMI READERS: 0

RELIGIONS

22 RELIGIOUS GROUPS:	PER CENT OF UNIT:	DECLINE/GROWTH:
A. PROTESTANT - Christian	1	Slow
B. ROMAN CATHOLIC	1	
C. ISLAM	10	Rapid
D. ANIMIST	85	Declining
E. INDEPENDENT CHURCHES	Nil	

23 PRESENT CHRISTIAN WITNESS: ECWA

24 ORGANISED/UNORGANISED CHURCHES WITH ADHERENTS FROM THIS UNIT:
   NAME   YEAR BEGUN   ADHERENTS   GROWTH TREND

25 ORGANISED CHURCHES WITH NO MEMBERS FROM THIS UNIT: No

26 EARLIEST KNOWN CHRISTIAN WITNESS: GROUP: YEAR:

27 OPENNESS TO RELIGIOUS CHANGE: Islam growing rapidly

28 PER CENT OF UNIT THAT HAS HEARD THE GOSPEL: Most %

29 MOST EFFECTIVE METHODS USED: A. Visit B. Literature C. Gospel teams

30 MEDIA MOST USED BY: YOUTH   ADULTS   STUDENTS   OTHERS

	YOUTH	ADULTS	STUDENTS	OTHERS
A. RADIO	x	x	x	
B. Books NEWSPAPER	x		x	
C. Bible	x	x	x	

31 FACTORS ENCOURAGING TO SPREAD OF CHRISTIANITY: Clinics MOre effort in
                                                                    witness
32 FACTORS HINDERING SPREAD OF CHRISTIANITY: Few take it seriously: Religious
   rites/Beer drinking/marriage customs
33 ATTITUDE TOWARD CHRISTIANITY: Reluctant

34 AREA OF PRESENT CONCENTRATION: West and Central

35 KIND OF PEOPLE BEING CONVERTED: Mature adults, youth

36 KIND OF PEOPLE BECOMING CHURCH LEADERS: Same as 35

37 QUALIFICATIONS OF PRESENT CHURCH LEADERSHIP: Four-year training

38 MUSLIM INFLUENCE: (RATING SCALE 1 low - 5 very strong)
      POLITICS 3-4 ECONOMY 4 SOCIAL 3 RELIGION   5
39 DESIRABILITY TO BECOME A MUSLIM: 4   WHICH SOCIAL GROUP: Elders, Youth

SCRIPTURE

40 LITERATURE PUBLISHED IN VERNACULAR: Nil DATE: IN PROCESS: Nil

41 CAN THEY READ SCRIPTURES IN ANOTHER LANGUAGE: Hausa

42 WHAT NEEDS EXIST THAT RELATE TO SCRIPTURES: 4,000 copies of any tract
   Illiteracy/   or book

COMMENTS:

43. ATTITUDE TOWARD GOSPEL - 2

44. PRIORITY - 1

IDENTIFICATION

1 GROUP NAME: Afo   Eloyi   2 POPULATION: 25,000

3 STATE/DIVISION Plateau/Nasarawa   4 ADMINISTRATIVE CENTRE : Nasarawa

5 LOCATION: N-Gbari/ E-Alago, Tiv/ S-Benue R/W-Gede/SE of Nasarawa

6 DESCRIPTION: A Village   B Agric.   C

                         D   E

7 ACCESSIBILITY: Semi-isolated, roads, trails, river

8 COMMUNICATION MEDIA: Radio, Post Office

9 DYNAMICS OF UNIT: Growing

10 INTERMARRIAGE:

11 PART OF LARGER UNIT, NAME: RELATIONSHIP:

12 POPULATION CENTRES / MARKET (M) / SCHOOL (S)
         Oedgi (S)
         Loko
         Rafin Gabas
13 FARM CROPS: G. Corn, sesame, maize, rice beans, tobacco, cotton

14 MEDICAL FACILITIES:

LANGUAGE / LITERACY

15 PRINCIPAL VERNACULAR: Afo   16 TRADE LANGUAGE: Hausa   75 % USERS

17 LITERATE ADULTS: 5%   18 CHANGE IN LITERACY RATE: Increasing slowly
                                                       (a backward tribe)
19 PER CENT CHRISTIANS WHO ARE LITERATE: %

20 WHAT DO PEOPLE READ: Bible, Newspaper

21 ESTIMATED ALJEMI READERS:

RELIGIONS

22 RELIGIOUS GROUPS: PER CENT OF UNIT: DECLINE/GROWTH:
    A. PROTESTANT   -1%   slow growth
    B. ROMAN CATHOLIC   slow growth
    C. ISLAM   5%
    D. ANIMIST   95%
    E. INDEPENDENT CHURCHES
23 PRESENT CHRISTIAN WITNESS: ECWA/Brethren from Agatu

24 ORGANISED/UNORGANISED CHURCHES WITH ADHERENTS FROM THIS UNIT:
   NAME   YEAR BEGUN   ADHERENTS   GROWTH TREND

        ECWA   1960?   100?   Slow growth

25 ORGANISED CHURCHES WITH NO MEMBERS FROM THIS UNIT:

26 EARLIEST KNOWN CHRISTIAN WITNESS: GROUP: SIM/ECWA   YEAR: 1960

27 OPENNESS TO RELIGIOUS CHANGE: Favorable

28 PER CENT OF UNIT THAT HAS HEARD THE GOSPEL: 25-30   %

29 MOST EFFECTIVE METHODS USED: A. Visitation   B. Open air preaching

30 MEDIA MOST USED BY: YOUTH   ADULTS   STUDENTS   OTHERS
   A. RADIO   x   x   x
   B. NEWSPAPER
   C. Literature   x   x

31 FACTORS ENCOURAGING TO SPREAD OF CHRISTIANITY: Lack of Islamic influence

32 FACTORS HINDERING SPREAD OF CHRISTIANITY: Strong idolatry, system of
   exchange marriage and polygamy.
33 ATTITUDE TOWARD CHRISTIANITY: Favorable

34 AREA OF PRESENT CONCENTRATION: Hills, (Plains to River Benue neglected)

35 KIND OF PEOPLE BEING CONVERTED: Youth

36 KIND OF PEOPLE BECOMING CHURCH LEADERS: Youth adults

37 QUALIFICATIONS OF PRESENT CHURCH LEADERSHIP:

38 MUSLIM INFLUENCE: (RATING SCALE 1 low - 5 very strong)
      POLITICS 3   ECONOMY 2 SOCIAL 2   RELIGION 2

39 DESIRABILITY TO BECOME A MUSLIM: 2   WHICH SOCIAL GROUP:

SCRIPTURE

40 LITERATURE PUBLISHED IN VERNACULAR: DATE: IN PROCESS:
   A few pamphlets

41 CAN THEY READ SCRIPTURES IN ANOTHER LANGUAGE: Hausa

42 WHAT NEEDS EXIST THAT RELATE TO SCRIPTURES:
   Illiteracy no scripture in process

COMMENTS:

   43. ATTITUDE TOWARD GOSPEL - 4

   44. PRIORITY - 1

IDENTIFICATION

1 GROUP NAME: Bassa   Bassa Kwomu   **2 POPULATION:** 100,000 (SIL)

3 STATE/DIVISION   **4 ADMINISTRATIVE CENTRE :**
Plateau/Nasarawa, Kwara/Lokoja   Lokoja, Nasarawa
5 LOCATION: N & S Banks Benue R.   Near Niger R.

6 DESCRIPTION: A Eth-Ling   **B** small villages   **C** Agric.

                         D Lower class   **E** Stationary

7 ACCESSIBILITY: Semi isolated   River, road, trails

8 COMMUNICATION MEDIA: Postal S.F. Benve

9 DYNAMICS OF UNIT: Growing; young are restless; elders resist change

10 INTERMARRIAGE: No

11 PART OF LARGER UNIT, NAME: No   **RELATIONSHIP:**

12 POPULATION CENTRES / MARKET (M) / SCHOOL (S)
  <u>S</u> Dekina Odenyi Odugbo Sheriya Ikpece Ozugbe Ikende Atejukulo Ogane Neg
    M-S   M-S   M-S   M-S   M   M   M-S   M-S   M-S
   Korika-S Ogumba-S Ayede-S Akakana-S <u>N</u> Umalsha (M-s) Uzy (M-s) Kanyehu-S
13 FARM CROPS: Kahoto-S Sheje-S

14 MEDICAL FACILITIES: S: 6 Dispensaries 1 hospital; N: Dispensary
                          N.A. 3; QIM 1

LANGUAGE / LITERACY

15 PRINCIPAL VERNACULAR: Bassa   **16 TRADE LANGUAGE:** Hausa   10 **%** USERS
                                                           women, children
17 LITERATE ADULTS: 5 %   **18 CHANGE IN LITERACY RATE:** +   men do <u>not</u>

19 PER CENT CHRISTIANS WHO ARE LITERATE: 10-25 %

20 WHAT DO PEOPLE READ: Bible, Gaskiya Books

21 ESTIMATED ALJEMI READERS: None

RELIGIONS

22 RELIGIOUS GROUPS: PER CENT OF UNIT: DECLINE/GROWTH:

  A. PROTESTANT (Christian)   5-15   slow growth
  B. ROMAN CATHOLIC   2   slow growth
  C. ISLAM   1   stationary
  D. ANIMIST   80-90   declining
  E. INDEPENDENT CHURCHES   None

23 PRESENT CHRISTIAN WITNESS: Brethern Assemblies, Q.I.M., Anglican, Baptist

24 ORGANISED/UNORGANISED CHURCHES WITH ADHERENTS FROM THIS UNIT:

NAME	YEAR BEGUN	ADHERENTS	GROWTH TREND
A. Brethern Assemblies	1945	2,000	Slow growth
B. Q.I.M.		450	Growing
C. Anglican, ECWA, Baptist			

25 ORGANISED CHURCHES WITH NO MEMBERS FROM THIS UNIT: ECWA (Gbari)

26 EARLIEST KNOWN CHRISTIAN WITNESS: GROUP: S.U.M.   YEAR: 1910

27 OPENNESS TO RELIGIOUS CHANGE:

28 PER CENT OF UNIT THAT HAS HEARD THE GOSPEL: Almost all

29 MOST EFFECTIVE METHODS USED: A. Gospel teams Records/cassettes B. Bible studies markets c. Visitation CRI teachers

30 MEDIA MOST USED BY:

	YOUTH	ADULTS	STUDENTS	OTHERS
A. RADIO	x	x	x	
B. LEAFLETS	x	x	x	Books
C. SCRIPTURES	x		x	Mags.

31 FACTORS ENCOURAGING TO SPREAD OF CHRISTIANITY: Christian family units/reading classes/help people in need transformed lives

32 FACTORS HINDERING SPREAD OF CHRISTIANITY: Denominational confusion and lack of cooperation

33 ATTITUDE TOWARD CHRISTIANITY: Indifferent

34 AREA OF PRESENT CONCENTRATION: N and S of Benue R.

35 KIND OF PEOPLE BEING CONVERTED:S: Mature adults   N: Youth, children

36 KIND OF PEOPLE BECOMING CHURCH LEADERS: See #35

37 QUALIFICATIONS OF PRESENT CHURCH LEADERSHIP: 3-4 years training/untrained

38 MUSLIM INFLUENCE: (RATING SCALE 1 low - 5 very strong)
   POLITICS 3   ECONOMY 3 SOCIAL 3 RELIGION 2-3

39 DESIRABILITY TO BECOME A MUSLIM: N:Yes WHICH SOCIAL GROUP: All
   Reason: Social economic & prestige/ S: No

SCRIPTURE

40 LITERATURE PUBLISHED IN VERNACULAR: DATE: IN PROCESS: O.T. Books
                              N.T.   1972 Gospels Portions O.T.

41 CAN THEY READ SCRIPTURES IN ANOTHER LANGUAGE: Hausa Bible

42 WHAT NEEDS EXIST THAT RELATE TO SCRIPTURES: Few can read Bass/complete Bible
   Illiteracy, until recently lack of motivation to read

COMMENTS:

43. ATTITUDE TOWARD GOSPEL - 4

44. PRIORITY - 1

IDENTIFICATION

1 GROUP NAME: Gade   Gede   2 POPULATION: 25,000

3 STATE/DIVISION Plateau/Nasarawa   4 ADMINISTRATIVE CENTRE : Nasarawa

5 LOCATION: W of Nasarawa/Gbari, Bassa - S Afo SE

6 DESCRIPTION: A Ethno-Ling   B Agric   C Villages

                D   E

7 ACCESSIBILITY: Road trails

8 COMMUNICATION MEDIA: Postal

9 DYNAMICS OF UNIT: Increasing   changing

10 INTERMARRIAGE:

11 PART OF LARGER UNIT, NAME: RELATIONSHIP:

12 POPULATION CENTRES / MARKET (M) / SCHOOL (S)

                Ara

13 FARM CROPS: Maize, g. corn, yams, millet, cotton, rice, cassava, cotton

14 MEDICAL FACILITIES:

LANGUAGE / LITERACY

15 PRINCIPAL VERNACULAR: Gade   16 TRADE LANGUAGE: Hausa   % USERS

17 LITERATE ADULTS: few %   18 CHANGE IN LITERACY RATE:

19 PER CENT CHRISTIANS WHO ARE LITERATE: %

20 WHAT DO PEOPLE READ:

21 ESTIMATED ALJEMI READERS: None

RELIGIONS

22 RELIGIOUS GROUPS:	PER CENT OF UNIT:	DECLINE/GROWTH:
A. PROTESTANT	1%	slow growth
B. ROMAN CATHOLIC		
C. ISLAM	98%	slow decline
D. ANIMIST		
E. INDEPENDENT CHURCHES		

23 PRESENT CHRISTIAN WITNESS: ECWA at Ara and outstations

24 ORGANISED/UNORGANISED CHURCHES WITH ADHERENTS FROM THIS UNIT:

NAME	YEAR BEGUN	ADHERENTS	GROWTH TREND
ECWA	c. 1960		slow growth

25 ORGANISED CHURCHES WITH NO MEMBERS FROM THIS UNIT:

26 EARLIEST KNOWN CHRISTIAN WITNESS: GROUP: S.I.M.   YEAR:

27 OPENNESS TO RELIGIOUS CHANGE: Signs of change

28 PER CENT OF UNIT THAT HAS HEARD THE GOSPEL: 50%

29 MOST EFFECTIVE METHODS USED:

30 MEDIA MOST USED BY: YOUTH   ADULTS   STUDENTS   OTHERS
   A. RADIO
   B. NEWSPAPER
   C.

31 FACTORS ENCOURAGING TO SPREAD OF CHRISTIANITY:

32 FACTORS HINDERING SPREAD OF CHRISTIANITY: Gade do not mix with Gbari
     Not enough concentration on this group
33 ATTITUDE TOWARD CHRISTIANITY:

34 AREA OF PRESENT CONCENTRATION:

35 KIND OF PEOPLE BEING CONVERTED: Youth

36 KIND OF PEOPLE BECOMING CHURCH LEADERS:

37 QUALIFICATIONS OF PRESENT CHURCH LEADERSHIP: 1 - 2 years training

38 MUSLIM INFLUENCE: (RATING SCALE 1 low - 5 very strong)
      POLITICS   ECONOMY   SOCIAL   RELIGION
39 DESIRABILITY TO BECOME A MUSLIM: WHICH SOCIAL GROUP:

SCRIPTURE

40 LITERATURE PUBLISHED IN VERNACULAR: DATE: IN PROCESS:
                 None

41 CAN THEY READ SCRIPTURES IN ANOTHER LANGUAGE: Hausa

42 WHAT NEEDS EXIST THAT RELATE TO SCRIPTURES:

COMMENTS:

43. ATTITUDE TOWARD GOSPEL: - 4

44. PRIORITY - 1

<u>IDENTIFICATION</u>

1 GROUP NAME: Gwandara   **2 POPULATION:** 25.000 (SIL)

3 STATE/DIVISION Plateau/Keffi Nasarawa**ADMINISTRATIVE CENTRE :** Keffi

5 LOCATION: Scattered Karshi to Eggon/Gbari, Gade

6 DESCRIPTION: **A** Ethno-Ling **B** Agric.   **C** Villages

                  D   **E**

7 ACCESSIBILITY: Some isolated remote areas

8 COMMUNICATION MEDIA:

9 DYNAMICS OF UNIT:

10 INTERMARRIAGE: Maintained identity although scattered

11 PART OF LARGER UNIT, NAME: **RELATIONSHIP:**

12 POPULATION CENTRES / MARKET (M) / SCHOOL (S)
     Karshi   Gudi   7 schools in area (1968)
     Keffi
13 FARM CROPS: G. corn, rice, millet, yams, okra, cotton, beniseed

14 MEDICAL FACILITIES: Hospital Keffi

<u>LANGUAGE / LITERACY</u>

15 PRINCIPAL VERNACULAR: Gwandara   **16 TRADE LANGUAGE:** Hausa   **%** USERS
                            (similar to Hausa)
17 LITERATE ADULTS: few **%**   **18 CHANGE IN LITERACY RATE:** None

19 PER CENT CHRISTIANS WHO ARE LITERATE: **%**

20 WHAT DO PEOPLE READ:

21 ESTIMATED ALJEMI READERS:

<u>RELIGIONS</u>

22 RELIGIOUS GROUPS: **PER CENT OF UNIT:**   **DECLINE/GROWTH:**
    A. PROTESTANT
    B. ROMAN CATHOLIC
    C. ISLAM
    D. ANIMIST   99%
    E. INDEPENDENT CHURCHES
23 PRESENT CHRISTIAN WITNESS: ECWA and Baptist

24 ORGANISED/UNORGANISED CHURCHES WITH ADHERENTS FROM THIS UNIT:
   NAME   YEAR BEGUN   ADHERENTS   GROWTH TREND

25 ORGANISED CHURCHES WITH NO MEMBERS FROM THIS UNIT: ECWA - Baptist

26 EARLIEST KNOWN CHRISTIAN WITNESS: GROUP: YEAR:

27 OPENNESS TO RELIGIOUS CHANGE:

28 PER CENT OF UNIT THAT HAS HEARD THE GOSPEL: 25 %

29 MOST EFFECTIVE METHODS USED:

30 MEDIA MOST USED BY: YOUTH   ADULTS   STUDENTS   OTHERS
   A. RADIO
   B. NEWSPAPER
   C.

31 FACTORS ENCOURAGING TO SPREAD OF CHRISTIANITY: Churches among Gbari Mada
   Yiskwa believers reaching out to them
32 FACTORS HINDERING SPREAD OF CHRISTIANITY: Very strong traditional religion
   with high degree of idolatry. More workers need to concentrate
33 ATTITUDE TOWARD CHRISTIANITY: Restraint

34 AREA OF PRESENT CONCENTRATION:

35 KIND OF PEOPLE BEING CONVERTED:

36 KIND OF PEOPLE BECOMING CHURCH LEADERS:

37 QUALIFICATIONS OF PRESENT CHURCH LEADERSHIP: No Gwandara church as such

38 MUSLIM INFLUENCE: (RATING SCALE 1 low - 5 very strong)
   POLITICS 4   ECONOMY 3 SOCIAL 3 RELIGION 3
39 DESIRABILITY TO BECOME A MUSLIM: 2   WHICH SOCIAL GROUP:

SCRIPTURE
40 LITERATURE PUBLISHED IN VERNACULAR: DATE: IN PROCESS:

41 CAN THEY READ SCRIPTURES IN ANOTHER LANGUAGE: Hausa

42 WHAT NEEDS EXIST THAT RELATE TO SCRIPTURES: Literacy

COMMENTS:

   43. ATTITUDE TOWARD GOSPEL - 2

   44. PRIORITY FOR ACTION - 1

IDENTIFICATION

1 GROUP NAME: Busa   2 POPULATION: 50,000 (SIL)

3 STATE/DIVISION Kwara, Borg u   4 ADMINISTRATIVE CENTRE : New Bussa

5 LOCATION: N.E. Niger River, Hausa, Kambara, W. Dahomey, Boko Bariba,
            S. Yoruba
6 DESCRIPTION: A Eth Ling   B Agric.   C Fishing

                 D Small villages E

7 ACCESSIBILITY: Semi isolated road trail

8 COMMUNICATION MEDIA: Postal radio

9 DYNAMICS OF UNIT: Stable Resisting change

10 INTERMARRIAGE: Yes

11 PART OF LARGER UNIT, NAME: RELATIONSHIP:

12 POPULATION CENTRES / MARKET (M) / SCHOOL (S)
   Kaiama M · PS   New Bussa   M S2 Wawa M TC

13 FARM CROPS: Yams, g. corn, g. nuts, cotton

14 MEDICAL FACILITIES: Hospital N. Bussa   2. Clincis Kaima Wawa

LANGUAGE / LITERACY

15 PRINCIPAL VERNACULAR: Busa   16 TRADE LANGUAGE: Hausa   40 % USERS
                        (Bokobarn Akiba)
17 LITERATE ADULTS: 2 %   18 CHANGE IN LITERACY RATE: Increasing

19 PER CENT CHRISTIANS WHO ARE LITERATE: 1 %

20 WHAT DO PEOPLE READ: Newspaper, Bible, Gaskiya books

21 ESTIMATED ALJEMI READERS: many in towns

RELIGIONS

22 RELIGIOUS GROUPS: PER CENT OF UNIT: DECLINE/GROWTH:
   A. PROTESTANT (Christian)   1%   slow growth

   B. ROMAN CATHOLIC

   C. ISLAM   50%   increasing

   D. ANIMIST   50%   decline

   E. INDEPENDENT CHURCHES

23 PRESENT CHRISTIAN WITNESS: Methodist

24 ORGANISED/UNORGANISED CHURCHES WITH ADHERENTS FROM THIS UNIT:

NAME	YEAR BEGUN	ADHERENTS	GROWTH TREND
Methodist	1963	544	Growing

25 ORGANISED CHURCHES WITH NO MEMBERS FROM THIS UNIT: Anglican, CAC, Apostolic, Baptist, RC (Yoruba)

26 EARLIEST KNOWN CHRISTIAN WITNESS: GROUP: Methodist   YEAR: 1939

27 OPENNESS TO RELIGIOUS CHANGE: 1959 many decided for Islam

28 PER CENT OF UNIT THAT HAS HEARD THE GOSPEL: few   %

29 MOST EFFECTIVE METHODS USED: Teams of agric health literacy evangelist - (4)

30 MEDIA MOST USED BY:

	YOUTH	ADULTS	STUDENTS	OTHERS
A. RADIO	x	x	x	Newspapers
B. LEAFLETS/ POSTERS	x	x	x	Magazines
C. SCRIPTURES	x	x	x	

31 FACTORS ENCOURAGING TO SPREAD OF CHRISTIANITY: Education, Health, Films, Preaching

32 FACTORS HINDERING SPREAD OF CHRISTIANITY:

33 ATTITUDE TOWARD CHRISTIANITY: Reluctant

34 AREA OF PRESENT CONCENTRATION:

35 KIND OF PEOPLE BEING CONVERTED: Adults, Youth, Women

36 KIND OF PEOPLE BECOMING CHURCH LEADERS: Mature adults

37 QUALIFICATIONS OF PRESENT CHURCH LEADERSHIP: 1 year training

38 MUSLIM INFLUENCE: (RATING SCALE 1 low - 5 very strong)
POLITICS 5 ECONOMY 3 SOCIAL 5 RELIGION

39 DESIRABILITY TO BECOME A MUSLIM: WHICH SOCIAL GROUP:

SCRIPTURE

40 LITERATURE PUBLISHED IN VERNACULAR: DATE: IN PROCESS:
Portions 1971 (Mark)

41 CAN THEY READ SCRIPTURES IN ANOTHER LANGUAGE: Hausa

42 WHAT NEEDS EXIST THAT RELATE TO SCRIPTURES: N.T. Stories tracts illiteracy

COMMENTS:

43. ATTITUDE TOWARD GOSPEL - 2

44. PRIORITY FOR ACTION - 1

IDENTIFICATION

1 GROUP NAME: Igbirra   2 POPULATION:

3 STATE/DIVISION Kwara State   4 ADMINISTRATIVE CENTRE : Okene

5 LOCATION: (North - Kogi Division: West - Kabba Division: South - Midwest)
             East - Igala Division
6 DESCRIPTION: A Tribe   B Towns   C Agric.

               D Middle class E Middle income . All over Nigeria: esp.
                                                    Northern and Western States

7 ACCESSIBILITY: Easily; road

8 COMMUNICATION MEDIA: Postal

9 DYNAMICS OF UNIT: Growing   Stable

10 INTERMARRIAGE: Accepted by in unit

11 PART OF LARGER UNIT, NAME: No   RELATIONSHIP:

12 POPULATION CENTRES / MARKET (M) / SCHOOL (S) Okene; Adaba; Ihima Districts
   Okene ·(MP; Gaminana (M); Okengwe (m); Many Pri. Schools; Atta College:
   Fed. Adv. Teach. College

13 FARM CROPS: Yams, cassava, g. corn, g. nuts

14 MEDICAL FACILITIES: Dispensaries, General Hospital, clinics (2) Maternities

LANGUAGE / LITERACY

15 PRINCIPAL VERNACULAR: Igbirra   16 TRADE LANGUAGE: No   % USERS

17 LITERATE ADULTS: 25 %   18 CHANGE IN LITERACY RATE: Increasing

19 PER CENT CHRISTIANS WHO ARE LITERATE: ? %

20 WHAT DO PEOPLE READ: Newspaper, Bible

21 ESTIMATED ALJEMI READERS: ?

RELIGIONS

22 RELIGIOUS GROUPS: PER CENT OF UNIT: DECLINE/GROWTH:
   A. PROTESTANT (Christian)   8%   slow growth
   B. ROMAN CATHOLIC   12%   stationary
   C. ISLAM   70%   stationary
   D. ANIMIST   10%   stationary
   E. INDEPENDENT CHURCHES

23 PRESENT CHRISTIAN WITNESS: ECWA, Anglican, Baptist, Pentecost

24 ORGANISED/UNORGANISED CHURCHES WITH ADHERENTS FROM THIS UNIT:
   <u>NAME</u>   YEAR BEGUN   ADHERENTS   GROWTH TREND
   Anglican   Slow
   ECWA and Baptist   Slow
                        Pentecost   Moderate
25 ORGANISED CHURCHES WITH NO MEMBERS FROM THIS UNIT:

26 EARLIEST KNOWN CHRISTIAN WITNESS: GROUP: RCM; CMS: SIM/ECWA YEAR:

27 OPENNESS TO RELIGIOUS CHANGE: Yes

28 PER CENT OF UNIT THAT HAS HEARD THE GOSPEL: All   %
                                  (a)   (b)
29 MOST EFFECTIVE METHODS USED: House visitation and market preach

30 MEDIA MOST USED BY: YOUTH   ADULTS   STUDENTS   OTHERS
   A. RADIO
   B. NEWSPAPER   All Media   x
   C.

31 FACTORS ENCOURAGING TO SPREAD OF CHRISTIANITY: Christian schools,
                                                 Youth centers & Clubs
32 FACTORS HINDERING SPREAD OF CHRISTIANITY:

33 ATTITUDE TOWARD CHRISTIANITY: Somewhat favorable

34 AREA OF PRESENT CONCENTRATION: West

35 KIND OF PEOPLE BEING CONVERTED: Women

36 KIND OF PEOPLE BECOMING CHURCH LEADERS:

37 QUALIFICATIONS OF PRESENT CHURCH LEADERSHIP:

38 MUSLIM INFLUENCE: (RATING SCALE 1 low - 5 very strong)
      POLITICS 4   ECONOMY 3   SOCIAL 4   RELIGION 3
39 DESIRABILITY TO BECOME A MUSLIM: WHICH SOCIAL GROUP:

SCRIPTURE

40 LITERATURE PUBLISHED IN VERNACULAR: DATE: IN PROCESS:
      Portions New Testament

41 CAN THEY READ SCRIPTURES IN ANOTHER LANGUAGE:

42 WHAT NEEDS EXIST THAT RELATE TO SCRIPTURES:
      Scripture translation in vernacular

COMMENTS:

   43. ATTITUDE TOWARD GOSPEL - 2

   44. PRIORITY FOR.ACTION - 2-3

IDENTIFICATION

1 GROUP NAME: Hausa Maguzawa   **2 POPULATION:** 100,000 (SIL)

3 STATE/DIVISION Kano/Kaduna/Sokoto   **4 ADMINISTRATIVE CENTRE :** Kano

5 LOCATION: Scattered throughout

6 DESCRIPTION: A Agric.   **B** Family units   **C**

             D   **E**

7 ACCESSIBILITY: Away from main roads, trails

8 COMMUNICATION MEDIA:

9 DYNAMICS OF UNIT: Growing moving toward radical change

10 INTERMARRIAGE: No

11 PART OF LARGER UNIT, NAME: **RELATIONSHIP:**

12 POPULATION CENTRES / MARKET (M) / SCHOOL (S)

13 FARM CROPS: G. corn, millet, g. nuts, cotton, maize

14 MEDICAL FACILITIES:

LANGUAGE / LITERACY

15 PRINCIPAL VERNACULAR: Hausa   **16 TRADE LANGUAGE:**   **% USERS**

17 LITERATE ADULTS: **%**   **18 CHANGE IN LITERACY RATE:** Increasing

19 PER CENT CHRISTIANS WHO ARE LITERATE: 50 **%**

20 WHAT DO PEOPLE READ:

21 ESTIMATED ALJEMI READERS: None

RELIGIONS

22 RELIGIOUS GROUPS: **PER CENT OF UNIT:**   **DECLINE/GROWTH:**
    A. PROTESTANT   1%
    B. ROMAN CATHOLIC
    C. ISLAM   99%
    D. ANIMIST
    E. INDEPENDENT CHURCHES

23 PRESENT CHRISTIAN WITNESS:

24 ORGANISED/UNORGANISED CHURCHES WITH ADHERENTS FROM THIS UNIT:

NAME	YEAR BEGUN	ADHERENTS	GROWTH TREND
a. ECWA	1936		
b. Anglican (CMS)	1920		
c. Baptist	1950		

25 ORGANISED CHURCHES WITH NO MEMBERS FROM THIS UNIT:

26 EARLIEST KNOWN CHRISTIAN WITNESS: GROUP: CMS   YEAR:

27 OPENNESS TO RELIGIOUS CHANGE: Very open, Family units becoming Christians

28 PER CENT OF UNIT THAT HAS HEARD THE GOSPEL: 10-25 %

29 MOST EFFECTIVE METHODS USED:

30 MEDIA MOST USED BY: YOUTH   ADULTS   STUDENTS   OTHERS

   A. RADIO

   B. NEWSPAPER

   C.

31 FACTORS ENCOURAGING TO SPREAD OF CHRISTIANITY: Large family groups

32 FACTORS HINDERING SPREAD OF CHRISTIANITY: Pressure from Islam

33 ATTITUDE TOWARD CHRISTIANITY: Favorable

34 AREA OF PRESENT CONCENTRATION: Northern Zaria, Southern Katsina

35 KIND OF PEOPLE BEING CONVERTED: Youth Adults

36 KIND OF PEOPLE BECOMING CHURCH LEADERS: Youth Adults

37 QUALIFICATIONS OF PRESENT CHURCH LEADERSHIP: Training 3-4 years

38 MUSLIM INFLUENCE: (RATING SCALE 1 low - 5 very strong)
   POLITICS 2 ECONOMY 3 SOCIAL 2 RELIGION 2

39 DESIRABILITY TO BECOME A MUSLIM: none   WHICH SOCIAL GROUP:

SCRIPTURE

40 LITERATURE PUBLISHED IN VERNACULAR: DATE: IN PROCESS:
   Hausa Bible 1932

41 CAN THEY READ SCRIPTURES IN ANOTHER LANGUAGE:

42 WHAT NEEDS EXIST THAT RELATE TO SCRIPTURES:

COMMENTS:

   43. ATTITUDE TOWARD GOSPEL - 4

   44. PRIORITY FOR ACTION - 1

IDENTIFICATION

1 GROUP NAME: Kadara   2 POPULATION: 40,000

3 STATE/DIVISION S of Kaduna/Ikulu- 4 ADMINISTRATIVE CENTRE :
S/ Gwari-W/ Ruruma-E In NW State/Minna Div.
5 LOCATION:

6 DESCRIPTION: A Ethno-Long   B Villages   C Agric.

                D Local village chiefs only

7 ACCESSIBILITY: Many remote areas/road, river, rail.

8 COMMUNICATION MEDIA: Radio, postal

9 DYNAMICS OF UNIT: Adopting new patterns

10 INTERMARRIAGE: Yes

11 PART OF LARGER UNIT, NAME: RELATIONSHIP:

12 POPULATION CENTRES / MARKET (M) / SCHOOL (S) Kufano M-Wed S Kalla M-Tu S
Kateri S Maro M-Fr Adunu M-4th day S Rima M-W Ishau M-W - S

13 FARM CROPS: G. corn, maize, rice, yams, cassava, beans, g. nuts, cotton

14 MEDICAL FACILITIES:

LANGUAGE / LITERACY

15 PRINCIPAL VERNACULAR: Kadara   16 TRADE LANGUAGE: Hausa   99% USERS

17 LITERATE ADULTS: 20 %   18 CHANGE IN LITERACY RATE:

19 PER CENT CHRISTIANS WHO ARE LITERATE: 60 %

20 WHAT DO PEOPLE READ: Gaskiya books, Bible

21 ESTIMATED ALJEMI READERS: Some in larger towns

RELIGIONS

22 RELIGIOUS GROUPS:	PER CENT OF UNIT:	DECLINE/GROWTH:
A. PROTESTANT	10%	Increasing
B. ROMAN CATHOLIC	5%	Slow growth
C. ISLAM	5%	Static
D. ANIMIST	80%	Declining
E. INDEPENDENT CHURCHES		

23 PRESENT CHRISTIAN WITNESS:

24 ORGANISED/UNORGANISED CHURCHES WITH ADHERENTS FROM THIS UNIT:

NAME	YEAR BEGUN	ADHERENTS	GROWTH TREND
ECWA	1950		Growing
Baptist	1960		Growing

25 ORGANISED CHURCHES WITH NO MEMBERS FROM THIS UNIT:

26 EARLIEST KNOWN CHRISTIAN WITNESS: GROUP: S.I.M.   YEAR: 1937

27 OPENNESS TO RELIGIOUS CHANGE: Favorable

28 PER CENT OF UNIT THAT HAS HEARD THE GOSPEL: 50-75 %

29 MOST EFFECTIVE METHODS USED: A. House visit B. Market gospel team
                                 C. Bible School   N.L.F.A. literature

30 MEDIA MOST USED BY:

	YOUTH	ADULTS	STUDENTS	OTHERS
A. RADIO	x	x	x	
SCRIPTURES	x	x	x	
B. NEWSPAPER				
C. BOOKS	x		x	

31 FACTORS ENCOURAGING TO SPREAD OF CHRISTIANITY: Kadara language   Rural
                                                                  development
32 FACTORS HINDERING SPREAD OF CHRISTIANITY: Idolatry, polygamy, alcoholism,
     lack of mobility for evangelism
33 ATTITUDE TOWARD CHRISTIANITY: Somewhat favorable

34 AREA OF PRESENT CONCENTRATION: North South / Central hinterlands are
                                                         neglected
35 KIND OF PEOPLE BEING CONVERTED: Youth

36 KIND OF PEOPLE BECOMING CHURCH LEADERS: Young adults

37 QUALIFICATIONS OF PRESENT CHURCH LEADERSHIP: Licensed 4-year training

38 MUSLIM INFLUENCE: (RATING SCALE 1 low - 5 very strong)
     POLITICS 4   ECONOMY 2 SOCIAL 2   RELIGION 3
39 DESIRABILITY TO BECOME A MUSLIM: Little WHICH SOCIAL GROUP: Elders

SCRIPTURE

40 LITERATURE PUBLISHED IN VERNACULAR: DATE: IN PROCESS:
          None

41 CAN THEY READ SCRIPTURES IN ANOTHER LANGUAGE: Hausa, English

42 WHAT NEEDS EXIST THAT RELATE TO SCRIPTURES: Illiteracy

COMMENTS:

43. ATTITUDE TOWARD GOSPEL - 5

44. PRIORITY FOR ACTION - 1

IDENTIFICATION

1 GROUP NAME: Afawa   Paawa   **2 POPULATION:** 10,000

3 STATE/DIVISION Bauchi/Ningi   **4 ADMINISTRATIVE CENTRE :** Ningi

5 LOCATION: Warjawa/ near Ningi/ N of Bunga Riv.

6 DESCRIPTION: **A** Ethno-LIng   **B** Villages   **C** Agric.

                     D   **E**

7 ACCESSIBILITY: Semi isolated, road, trails

8 COMMUNICATION MEDIA:

9 DYNAMICS OF UNIT:

10 INTERMARRIAGE:

11 PART OF LARGER UNIT, NAME: Yes Warjawa   **RELATIONSHIP:** Warjawa sub group

12 POPULATION CENTRES / MARKET (M) / SCHOOL (S) Ningi Ari S Tiffi S Tabila S
Kafin Zaki S Guda S

13 FARM CROPS:G corn, millet, maize, cotton, g. nuts, sugar cane

14 MEDICAL FACILITIES:Hospital Ningi

LANGUAGE / LITERACY

15 PRINCIPAL VERNACULAR: Afanci   **16 TRADE LANGUAGE:** Hausa   100 % USERS

17 LITERATE ADULTS: very few **18 CHANGE IN LITERACY RATE:** static

19 PER CENT CHRISTIANS WHO ARE LITERATE: %

20 WHAT DO PEOPLE READ:

21 ESTIMATED ALJEMI READERS:

RELIGIONS

22 RELIGIOUS GROUPS:	PER CENT OF UNIT:	DECLINE/GROWTH:
A. PROTESTANT	-1%	Static
B. ROMAN CATHOLIC		
C. ISLAM	20%	Growing
D. ANIMIST	80%	
E. INDEPENDENT CHURCHES		

23 PRESENT CHRISTIAN WITNESS: EMS evangelist Tiffi

24 ORGANISED/UNORGANISED CHURCHES WITH ADHERENTS FROM THIS UNIT:
   NAME   YEAR BEGUN   ADHERENTS   GROWTH TREND

   ECWA   1 family   static

25 ORGANISED CHURCHES WITH NO MEMBERS FROM THIS UNIT:

26 EARLIEST KNOWN CHRISTIAN WITNESS: GROUP: S.I.M.   YEAR: 1930's

27 OPENNESS TO RELIGIOUS CHANGE: Signs of change

28 PER CENT OF UNIT THAT HAS HEARD THE GOSPEL: %

29 MOST EFFECTIVE METHODS USED:

30 MEDIA MOST USED BY: YOUTH   ADULTS   STUDENTS   OTHERS
   A. RADIO
   B. NEWSPAPER
   C.

31 FACTORS ENCOURAGING TO SPREAD OF CHRISTIANITY: People are disillusioned
   with Islam: People show independence of Ningi influence
32 FACTORS HINDERING SPREAD OF CHRISTIANITY: Lack of evangelists

33 ATTITUDE TOWARD CHRISTIANITY: Favorable, dissatisfied with Islam

34 AREA OF PRESENT CONCENTRATION:

35 KIND OF PEOPLE BEING CONVERTED:

36 KIND OF PEOPLE BECOMING CHURCH LEADERS:

37 QUALIFICATIONS OF PRESENT CHURCH LEADERSHIP:

38 MUSLIM INFLUENCE: (RATING SCALE 1 low - 5 very strong)
      POLITICS 4 ECONOMY 3 SOCIAL 3 RELIGION 3

39 DESIRABILITY TO BECOME A MUSLIM: 3   WHICH SOCIAL GROUP: Young adults
SCRIPTURE

40 LITERATURE PUBLISHED IN VERNACULAR: DATE: IN PROCESS:

41 CAN THEY READ SCRIPTURES IN ANOTHER LANGUAGE: Hausa

42 WHAT NEEDS EXIST THAT RELATE TO SCRIPTURES: Literacy

COMMENTS:

   43. ATTITUDE TOWARD GOSPEL - 3

   44. PRIORITY FOR ACTION - 1

IDENTIFICATION

1 GROUP NAME: Buta   **2 POPULATION:** 20,000

3 STATE/DIVISION NE Kano, Ningi Div.   **4 ADMINISTRATIVE CENTRE :** Burra and Ningi

5 LOCATION: N.E./Kano Border   W of Ningi   Hausa/Afawa/Kurama

6 DESCRIPTION: A Rural   **B** Farmers   **C**

                 D   **E**

7 ACCESSIBILITY: Road track via Ningi dry season

8 COMMUNICATION MEDIA: Postal via Ningi   Radio

9 DYNAMICS OF UNIT: ?

10 INTERMARRIAGE: Little

11 PART OF LARGER UNIT, NAME: **RELATIONSHIP:**

12 POPULATION CENTRES / MARKET (M) / SCHOOL (S)
        Burra M/S   Yadda Gungume M/S

13 FARM CROPS: Maize, g. corn, g. nuts, cotton

14 MEDICAL FACILITIES: Disp.

LANGUAGE / LITERACY

15 PRINCIPAL VERNACULAR: Buta   **16 TRADE LANGUAGE:** Hausa   95 **% USERS**

17 LITERATE ADULTS: -2%   **18 CHANGE IN LITERACY RATE:** None

19 PER CENT CHRISTIANS WHO ARE LITERATE: 0%

20 WHAT DO PEOPLE READ:

21 ESTIMATED ALJEMI READERS:

RELIGIONS

22 RELIGIOUS GROUPS: **PER CENT OF UNIT:**   **DECLINE/GROWTH:**
    A. PROTESTANT
    B. ROMAN CATHOLIC
    C. ISLAM   60%   Slow growth
    D. ANIMIST   40%   Decline
    E. INDEPENDENT CHURCHES

23 PRESENT CHRISTIAN WITNESS: Nil/occasional Christian teacher

24 ORGANISED/UNORGANISED CHURCHES WITH ADHERENTS FROM THIS UNIT:
   <u>NAME</u>   <u>YEAR BEGUN</u>   <u>ADHERENTS</u>   <u>GROWTH TREND</u>
          Nil

25 ORGANISED CHURCHES WITH NO MEMBERS FROM THIS UNIT:

26 EARLIEST KNOWN CHRISTIAN WITNESS: GROUP: N.L.F.A. teams   YEAR: 1966

27 OPENNESS TO RELIGIOUS CHANGE:

28 PER CENT OF UNIT THAT HAS HEARD THE GOSPEL: -20 %
                                           No known Christians
29 MOST EFFECTIVE METHODS USED:
      Gospel teams   B. Lay evangelist

30 MEDIA MOST USED BY: YOUTH   ADULTS   STUDENTS   OTHERS
   A. RADIO
   B. NEWSPAPER
   C.

31 FACTORS ENCOURAGING TO SPREAD OF CHRISTIANITY: New Schools (U.P.E.)

32 FACTORS HINDERING SPREAD OF CHRISTIANITY: Lack of workers

33 ATTITUDE TOWARD CHRISTIANITY: Indifferent

34 AREA OF PRESENT CONCENTRATION:

35 KIND OF PEOPLE BEING CONVERTED:

36 KIND OF PEOPLE BECOMING CHURCH LEADERS:

37 QUALIFICATIONS OF PRESENT CHURCH LEADERSHIP:

38 MUSLIM INFLUENCE: (RATING SCALE 1 low - 5 very strong)
      POLITICS 4   ECONOMY 3 SOCIAL 3   RELIGION 2-3
39 DESIRABILITY TO BECOME A MUSLIM: 3   WHICH SOCIAL GROUP: Youth

<u>SCRIPTURE</u>

40 LITERATURE PUBLISHED IN VERNACULAR: DATE: IN PROCESS:
          Nil

41 CAN THEY READ SCRIPTURES IN ANOTHER LANGUAGE: Hausa

42 WHAT NEEDS EXIST THAT RELATE TO SCRIPTURES: Literacy

<u>COMMENTS:</u>

43. ATTITUDE TOWARD GOSPEL - 2

44. PRIORITY FOR·ACTION - 1

IDENTIFICATION

1 GROUP NAME: Warji   2 POPULATION: 70,000

3 STATE/DIVISION N.E. Ningi   4 ADMINISTRATIVE CENTRE : Bauchi

5 LOCATION: NE Ningi Dist. Along Bunga Riv.

6 DESCRIPTION: A Ethno-Ling   B Agri.   C Towns

                          D   E

7 ACCESSIBILITY: Road dry season

8 COMMUNICATION MEDIA: Radio

9 DYNAMICS OF UNIT: Stable

10 INTERMARRIAGE: Yes

11 PART OF LARGER UNIT, NAME: No   RELATIONSHIP:

12 POPULATION CENTRES / MARKET (M) / SCHOOL (S) Katanga (M-Tu) S Gasina (M-Su)
   Dagu ·S Tukunwada (M-Su) Bunga (M-Wed) Lirna S Rumba (M-Su) S Kadale (M-Th)

13 FARM CROPS: G. nuts, g. corn, millet, cassava, potato

14 MEDICAL FACILITIES: Clinic

LANGUAGE / LITERACY

15 PRINCIPAL VERNACULAR: Warji   16 TRADE LANGUAGE: Hausa 100 % USERS
                          (Diriyanci)
17 LITERATE ADULTS: 10%   ·18 CHANGE IN LITERACY RATE: Increasing

19 PER CENT CHRISTIANS WHO ARE LITERATE: 90%

20 WHAT DO PEOPLE READ:Gaskiya books, Bible

21 ESTIMATED ALJEMI READERS: Many in towns

RELIGIONS

22 RELIGIOUS GROUPS: PER CENT OF UNIT: DECLINE/GROWTH:
   A. PROTESTANT   1%   Slow growth
   B. ROMAN CATHOLIC
   C. ISLAM   50%   Stationary
   D. ANIMIST   50%   Decline
   E. INDEPENDENT CHURCHES None
23 PRESENT CHRISTIAN WITNESS: ECWA (SIM)

24 ORGANISED/UNORGANISED CHURCHES WITH ADHERENTS FROM THIS UNIT:

NAME	YEAR BEGUN	ADHERENTS	GROWTH TREND
ECWA	1930		

25 ORGANISED CHURCHES WITH NO MEMBERS FROM THIS UNIT: None

26 EARLIEST KNOWN CHRISTIAN WITNESS: GROUP: S.I.M.   YEAR: 1927-30

27 OPENNESS TO RELIGIOUS CHANGE: favorable

28 PER CENT OF UNIT THAT HAS HEARD THE GOSPEL: 25-50   %

29 MOST EFFECTIVE METHODS USED: A. Radio   B. House   C. Market

30 MEDIA MOST USED BY:

	YOUTH	ADULTS	STUDENTS	OTHERS
A. RADIO		Women		
B. POSTERS	x		x	
C. NEWS/MAGS			X	

31 FACTORS ENCOURAGING TO SPREAD OF CHRISTIANITY: Scripture in vernacular

32 FACTORS HINDERING SPREAD OF CHRISTIANITY: Absence of youth and women's
organizations

33 ATTITUDE TOWARD CHRISTIANITY: Favorable

34 AREA OF PRESENT CONCENTRATION: East

35 KIND OF PEOPLE BEING CONVERTED: Adults   youth

36 KIND OF PEOPLE BECOMING CHURCH LEADERS: Adults

37 QUALIFICATIONS OF PRESENT CHURCH LEADERSHIP: 3 years

38 MUSLIM INFLUENCE: (RATING SCALE 1 low - 5 very strong)
   POLITICS 4   ECONOMY 3 SOCIAL 2   RELIGION 5

39 DESIRABILITY TO BECOME A MUSLIM: 3   WHICH SOCIAL GROUP: Youth

SCRIPTURE

40 LITERATURE PUBLISHED IN VERNACULAR: DATE: IN PROCESS:
      No scripture

41 CAN THEY READ SCRIPTURES IN ANOTHER LANGUAGE: Hausa   English

42 WHAT NEEDS EXIST THAT RELATE TO SCRIPTURES: Translation to Warji

COMMENTS:

43. ATTITUTDE TOWARD GOSPEL - 2-3

44. PRIORITY FOR ACTION - 2

IDENTIFICATION

1 GROUP NAME: Miya Similar tribes: Jimbim,　**2 POPULATION:** 5,200 (SIL)
Siri,Tsagu

3 STATE/DIVISION N.E. / Bauchi　**4 ADMINISTRATIVE CENTRE :**

5 LOCATION: Ningi Road 44 miles north of Bauchi

6 DESCRIPTION: A Tribe　　　**B** Agri.　　　**C** Villages

　　　　　　　　D　　　　　**E**

7 ACCESSIBILITY: Easy road

8 COMMUNICATION MEDIA: None

9 DYNAMICS OF UNIT: stable

10 INTERMARRIAGE:

11 PART OF LARGER UNIT, NAME: No　　　**RELATIONSHIP:**

12 POPULATION CENTRES / MARKET (M) / SCHOOL (S) Jimbin Kafin Zaik Miya (m-Wed).
Ganjuwa Tando Maiwa　　　　　　　　　　　　　　　　　　S

13 FARM CROPS:

14 MEDICAL FACILITIES: ECWA dispensary

LANGUAGE / LITERACY

15 PRINCIPAL VERNACULAR: Miya　　**16 TRADE LANGUAGE:** Hausa　　**% USERS**

17 LITERATE ADULTS:　**%**　**18 CHANGE IN LITERACY RATE:** None

19 PER CENT CHRISTIANS WHO ARE LITERATE:　**%**

20 WHAT DO PEOPLE READ:

21 ESTIMATED ALJEMI READERS:

RELIGIONS

22 RELIGIOUS GROUPS:　　　　　　**PER CENT OF UNIT:**　**DECLINE/GROWTH:**
　　A. PROTESTANT　　　　　　　　　1-2%　　　　Slow growth
　　B. ROMAN CATHOLIC
　　C. ISLAM　　　　　　　　　　　-1%
　　D. ANIMIST　　　　　　　　　　98%
　　E. INDEPENDENT CHURCHES None

23 PRESENT CHRISTIAN WITNESS: ECWA church, dispensary

24 ORGANISED/UNORGANISED CHURCHES WITH ADHERENTS FROM THIS UNIT:

NAME	YEAR BEGUN	ADHERENTS	GROWTH TREND
ECWA	1961	60-100	Slow

25 ORGANISED CHURCHES WITH NO MEMBERS FROM THIS UNIT: None

26 EARLIEST KNOWN CHRISTIAN WITNESS: GROUP: S.I.M.   YEAR:

27 OPENNESS TO RELIGIOUS CHANGE:

28 PER CENT OF UNIT THAT HAS HEARD THE GOSPEL: 50 - 75 %

29 MOST EFFECTIVE METHODS USED: A. House B. Market C. Literature

30 MEDIA MOST USED BY: YOUTH   ADULTS   STUDENTS   OTHERS
   A. RADIO
   B. NEWSPAPER
   C.

31 FACTORS ENCOURAGING TO SPREAD OF CHRISTIANITY:

32 FACTORS HINDERING SPREAD OF CHRISTIANITY:

33 ATTITUDE TOWARD CHRISTIANITY: Reluctant

34 AREA OF PRESENT CONCENTRATION:

35 KIND OF PEOPLE BEING CONVERTED: Youth, Mature adults

36 KIND OF PEOPLE BECOMING CHURCH LEADERS:

37 QUALIFICATIONS OF PRESENT CHURCH LEADERSHIP: Licensed

38 MUSLIM INFLUENCE: (RATING SCALE 1 low - 5 very strong)
   POLITICS   ECONOMY   SOCIAL   RELIGION

39 DESIRABILITY TO BECOME A MUSLIM: No   WHICH SOCIAL GROUP:

SCRIPTURE

40 LITERATURE PUBLISHED IN VERNACULAR: None DATE: IN PROCESS: None

41 CAN THEY READ SCRIPTURES IN ANOTHER LANGUAGE: Hausa

42 WHAT NEEDS EXIST THAT RELATE TO SCRIPTURES:

COMMENTS:

43. ATTITUDE TOWARD GOSPEL - 3-4

44. PRIORITY FOR ACTION - 1

IDENTIFICATION

1 GROUP NAME: Jarawa includes Hill, Plain and   **2 POPULATION:** 150,000
smaller groups

3 STATE/DIVISION N.E. Bauchi   **4 ADMINISTRATIVE CENTRE :** Bauchi

5 LOCATION: E Jos/S. Bauchi

6 DESCRIPTION: A Ethno-Ling   **B**   Agric.   **C** Villages

                 D   **E**

7 ACCESSIBILITY: Semi isolatd trails roads

8 COMMUNICATION MEDIA:

9 DYNAMICS OF UNIT: Growing

10 INTERMARRIAGE:

11 PART OF LARGER UNIT, NAME: **RELATIONSHIP:**

12 POPULATION CENTRES / MARKET (M) / SCHOOL (S)

    Dass   Fobur
    Wurno   Lere
13 FARM CROPS: G. corn, millett, maize, g. nuts

14 MEDICAL FACILITIES:

LANGUAGE / LITERACY

15 PRINCIPAL VERNACULAR: Jaranci   **16 TRADE LANGUAGE:** Hausa   100% USERS

17 LITERATE ADULTS: %   **18 CHANGE IN LITERACY RATE:**

19 PER CENT CHRISTIANS WHO ARE LITERATE: 50 %

20 WHAT DO PEOPLE READ:

21 ESTIMATED ALJEMI READERS:

RELIGIONS

22 RELIGIOUS GROUPS:	**PER CENT OF UNIT:**	**DECLINE/GROWTH:**
A. PROTESTANT	10	(Mostly Hill and River J.)
B. ROMAN CATHOLIC		growing
C. ISLAM	20	
D. ANIMIST	70	
E. INDEPENDENT CHURCHES		

23 PRESENT CHRISTIAN WITNESS: ECWA   EKAS

24 ORGANISED/UNORGANISED CHURCHES WITH ADHERENTS FROM THIS UNIT:

NAME	YEAR BEGUN	ADHERENTS	GROWTH TREND
EKAS Plateau	1933		Increasing
ECWA	1930		Increasing

25 ORGANISED CHURCHES WITH NO MEMBERS FROM THIS UNIT:

26 EARLIEST KNOWN CHRISTIAN WITNESS: GROUP: Protestant   YEAR: 1930

27 OPENNESS TO RELIGIOUS CHANGE: People near Bauchi resistant

28 PER CENT OF UNIT THAT HAS HEARD THE GOSPEL: 50-75%

29 MOST EFFECTIVE METHODS USED:

30 MEDIA MOST USED BY: YOUTH   ADULTS   STUDENTS   OTHERS
  A. RADIO
  B. NEWSPAPER
  C.

31 FACTORS ENCOURAGING TO SPREAD OF CHRISTIANITY: Active gospel teams Awareness
of problems & where unevangelized areas are

32 FACTORS HINDERING SPREAD OF CHRISTIANITY:
Political fear and dominated by chiefs

33 ATTITUDE TOWARD CHRISTIANITY: Responsive to resistant

34 AREA OF PRESENT CONCENTRATION:

35 KIND OF PEOPLE BEING CONVERTED:

36 KIND OF PEOPLE BECOMING CHURCH LEADERS: Mature adults

37 QUALIFICATIONS OF PRESENT CHURCH LEADERSHIP: 3 - 4 years training

38 MUSLIM INFLUENCE: (RATING SCALE 1 low - 5 very strong)
  POLITICS 4   ECONOMY 3   SOCIAL 3   RELIGION 3

39 DESIRABILITY TO BECOME A MUSLIM: WHICH SOCIAL GROUP: Young adults

SCRIPTURE

40 LITERATURE PUBLISHED IN VERNACULAR: DATE: IN PROCESS:
  Gospels 1940

41 CAN THEY READ SCRIPTURES IN ANOTHER LANGUAGE: Hausa

42 WHAT NEEDS EXIST THAT RELATE TO SCRIPTURES: Literacy

COMMENTS:

43. ATTITUDE TOWARDS GOSPEL - 4

44. PRIORITY FOR ACTION - 3

IDENTIFICATION

1 GROUP NAME: Zaranda Hills Geji Belu Pelu Zul   **2 POPULATION:** 10,000
                    Girmawa Dulumi
3 STATE/DIVISION Bauchi   **4 ADMINISTRATIVE CENTRE :** Bauchi

5 LOCATION: N. of Jos--Bauchi Road

6 DESCRIPTION: A   **B**   **C**

                 D   **E**

7 ACCESSIBILITY: Semi isolated   road trail

8 COMMUNICATION MEDIA:

9 DYNAMICS OF UNIT: Stationary

10 INTERMARRIAGE:

11 PART OF LARGER UNIT, NAME: **RELATIONSHIP:**

12 POPULATION CENTRES / MARKET (M) / SCHOOL (S)
                 Napordo, Zul, Dulimi

13 FARM CROPS: G. corn, maize, millett, g. nuts, cotton

14 MEDICAL FACILITIES:

LANGUAGE / LITERACY

15 PRINCIPAL VERNACULAR: each its own **16 TRADE LANGUAGE:** Hausa   **% USERS**

17 LITERATE ADULTS: 1 %   **18 CHANGE IN LITERACY RATE:** Stationary

19 PER CENT CHRISTIANS WHO ARE LITERATE: %

20 WHAT DO PEOPLE READ:

21 ESTIMATED ALJEMI READERS:

RELIGIONS

22 RELIGIOUS GROUPS: **PER CENT OF UNIT:**   **DECLINE/GROWTH:**
   A. PROTESTANT   2%
   B. ROMAN CATHOLIC
   C. ISLAM
   D. ANIMIST   98%
   E. INDEPENDENT CHURCHES

23 PRESENT CHRISTIAN WITNESS: ECWA

24 ORGANISED/UNORGANISED CHURCHES WITH ADHERENTS FROM THIS UNIT:
   <u>NAME</u>   <u>YEAR BEGUN</u>   <u>ADHERENTS</u>   <u>GROWTH TREND</u>
      ECWA

25 ORGANISED CHURCHES WITH NO MEMBERS FROM THIS UNIT:

26 EARLIEST KNOWN CHRISTIAN WITNESS: GROUP: SIM   YEAR:

27 OPENNESS TO RELIGIOUS CHANGE: Reluctant

28 PER CENT OF UNIT THAT HAS HEARD THE GOSPEL: 25-50   %

29 MOST EFFECTIVE METHODS USED:

30 MEDIA MOST USED BY: YOUTH   ADULTS   STUDENTS   OTHERS
   A. RADIO
   B. NEWSPAPER
   C.

31 FACTORS ENCOURAGING TO SPREAD OF CHRISTIANITY: Churches along Bauchi
                                                 road are growing
32 FACTORS HINDERING SPREAD OF CHRISTIANITY: Difficult to get into area
                                             People hold on to customs
33 ATTITUDE TOWARD CHRISTIANITY: Favorable

34 AREA OF PRESENT CONCENTRATION: Zul - along motor road

35 KIND OF PEOPLE BEING CONVERTED:

36 KIND OF PEOPLE BECOMING CHURCH LEADERS:

37 QUALIFICATIONS OF PRESENT CHURCH LEADERSHIP:

38 MUSLIM INFLUENCE: (RATING SCALE 1 low - 5 very strong)
   POLITICS   ECONOMY   SOCIAL   RELIGION
39 DESIRABILITY TO BECOME A MUSLIM: 39   WHICH SOCIAL GROUP:

SCRIPTURE
   40 LITERATURE PUBLISHED IN VERNACULAR: DATE: IN PROCESS:

   41 CAN THEY READ SCRIPTURES IN ANOTHER LANGUAGE:

   42 WHAT NEEDS EXIST THAT RELATE TO SCRIPTURES:

COMMENTS:

   43. ATTITUDE TOWARD GOSPEL - 3

   44. PRIORITY FOR ACTION - 1

IDENTIFICATION

1 GROUP NAME: Babur Thali   Bura   **2 POPULATION:**

3 STATE/DIVISION Borno/Biu   **4 ADMINISTRATIVE CENTRE :** Biu

5 LOCATION: N and W. of Biu. Tera-S.W/ Karekare-N/Kanuri -NE Babur S

6 DESCRIPTION: A Village   **B** Agric.   **C** Stationary

                   D Fearful of   **E**
                       strangers
7 ACCESSIBILITY: Easy - roads

8 COMMUNICATION MEDIA: Radio

9 DYNAMICS OF UNIT: Growing stable   adopting new patterns

10 INTERMARRIAGE: Yes

11 PART OF LARGER UNIT, NAME: Yes   **RELATIONSHIP:** Babur Bura

12 POPULATION CENTRES / MARKET (M) / SCHOOL (S) Gulani M-S Gur Madagi M. Th
Garabila M Su S Gunda M-Su-S Bilarafa M-Wed-S Mandaragrau M Su S Titeba M Wed
Bara M-Tu

13 FARM CROPS: G. corn, onions, millet, cotton, g. nuts, maize, beans, rice

14 MEDICAL FACILITIES: Dispensary Gulani, Bilarafa

LANGUAGE / LITERACY

15 PRINCIPAL VERNACULAR: Bura (Babur) **16 TRADE LANGUAGE:** Hausa   **% USERS**

17 LITERATE ADULTS: 3 %   **18 CHANGE IN LITERACY RATE:** Decreasing

19 PER CENT CHRISTIANS WHO ARE LITERATE: 1%

20 WHAT DO PEOPLE READ: None

21 ESTIMATED ALJEMI READERS: A few in town

RELIGIONS

22 RELIGIOUS GROUPS: **PER CENT OF UNIT:**   **DECLINE/GROWTH:**

A. PROTESTANT	5%	Stationary
B. ROMAN CATHOLIC	None	
C. ISLAM	30-40%	Slow growth
D. ANIMIST	60%	Decline
E. INDEPENDENT CHURCHES	None	

23 PRESENT CHRISTIAN WITNESS: None today

24 ORGANISED/UNORGANISED CHURCHES WITH ADHERENTS FROM THIS UNIT:

NAME	YEAR BEGUN	ADHERENTS	GROWTH TREND
EKAS LG Prayer groups			

25 ORGANISED CHURCHES WITH NO MEMBERS FROM THIS UNIT: Eaka (EKAS LG)

26 EARLIEST KNOWN CHRISTIAN WITNESS: GROUP: EKAS LARDIN BAGAS (CBM) YEAR: 1947

27 OPENNESS TO RELIGIOUS CHANGE:Little change to Islam or Christianity

28 PER CENT OF UNIT THAT HAS HEARD THE GOSPEL: Very few %

29 MOST EFFECTIVE METHODS USED:A. Village evangelism B. Gospel team
   C. Evangelist

30 MEDIA MOST USED BY:

	YOUTH	ADULTS	STUDENTS	OTHERS
A. RADIO	x	x		
B. NEWSPAPER				
C.				

31 FACTORS ENCOURAGING TO SPREAD OF CHRISTIANITY: Farming with evangelism
   medicine with evangelism Bible pictures

32 FACTORS HINDERING SPREAD OF CHRISTIANITY:Lack of contact

33 ATTITUDE TOWARD CHRISTIANITY: Somewhat favorable

34 AREA OF PRESENT CONCENTRATION: None

35 KIND OF PEOPLE BEING CONVERTED: None

36 KIND OF PEOPLE BECOMING CHURCH LEADERS:

37 QUALIFICATIONS OF PRESENT CHURCH LEADERSHIP: None

38 MUSLIM INFLUENCE: (RATING SCALE 1 low - 5 very strong)
   POLITICS 3 ECONOMY 3 SOCIAL 3 RELIGION 3

39 DESIRABILITY TO BECOME A MUSLIM: Yes   WHICH SOCIAL GROUP: Family heads

SCRIPTURE

40 LITERATURE PUBLISHED IN VERNACULAR: DATE: IN PROCESS:
   N.T.   ?   Revision of N.T.

41 CAN THEY READ SCRIPTURES IN ANOTHER LANGUAGE:Hausa

42 WHAT NEEDS EXIST THAT RELATE TO SCRIPTURES: No Bura Bibles available -
   needed greatly

COMMENTS:

43. ATTITUDE TOWARD GOSPEL - 3-4

44. PRIORITY FOR ACTION - 1

<u>IDENTIFICATION</u>

1 GROUP NAME: Ngamawa   **2 POPULATION:** 10,000

3 STATE/DIVISION Borno/Fika - Bauchi **4 ADMINISTRATIVE CENTRE :** Potiskum

5 LOCATION: South of Potiskum to Gonala River

6 DESCRIPTION: A Villages   **B** Agric.   **C** Ethno-Ling

                 D   **E**

7 ACCESSIBILITY: Semi Isolated/Road/Trails

8 COMMUNICATION MEDIA: Radio

9 DYNAMICS OF UNIT:

10 INTERMARRIAGE:

11 PART OF LARGER UNIT, NAME: **RELATIONSHIP:**

12 POPULATION CENTRES / MARKET (M) / SCHOOL (S) Gandaka   Gudeili JIgawa
       Malor   Nahuta

13 FARM CROPS: G. corn, g. nuts, cotton, maize, millet

14 MEDICAL FACILITIES:

<u>LANGUAGE / LITERACY</u>

15 PRINCIPAL VERNACULAR: Ngamo   **16 TRADE LANGUAGE:** Hausa   **% USERS**

17 LITERATE ADULTS: **% 18 CHANGE IN LITERACY RATE:**

19 PER CENT CHRISTIANS WHO ARE LITERATE: 25 **%**

20 WHAT DO PEOPLE READ:

21 ESTIMATED ALJEMI READERS: Some in towns

<u>RELIGIONS</u>

22 RELIGIOUS GROUPS:	PER CENT OF UNIT:	DECLINE/GROWTH:
A. PROTESTANT	5%	Slow growth
B. ROMAN CATHOLIC	3%	Moderate
C. ISLAM	10%	Slow growth
D. ANIMIST	80-85%	
E. INDEPENDENT CHURCHES		

23 PRESENT CHRISTIAN WITNESS: LCWA

24 ORGANISED/UNORGANISED CHURCHES WITH ADHERENTS FROM THIS UNIT:

NAME	YEAR BEGUN	ADHERENTS	GROWTH TREND
ECWA	1960		Slow growth

25 ORGANISED CHURCHES WITH NO MEMBERS FROM THIS UNIT:

26 EARLIEST KNOWN CHRISTIAN WITNESS: GROUP: S.I.M   YEAR: 1942

27 OPENNESS TO RELIGIOUS CHANGE: Open   RC gaining rapidly

28 PER CENT OF UNIT THAT HAS HEARD THE GOSPEL: 50 %

29 MOST EFFECTIVE METHODS USED:

30 MEDIA MOST USED BY: YOUTH   ADULTS   STUDENTS   OTHERS
   A. RADIO
   B. NEWSPAPER
   C.

31 FACTORS ENCOURAGING TO SPREAD OF CHRISTIANITY:

32 FACTORS HINDERING SPREAD OF CHRISTIANITY:

33 ATTITUDE TOWARD CHRISTIANITY: Somewhat favorable

34 AREA OF PRESENT CONCENTRATION: Gadaka

35 KIND OF PEOPLE BEING CONVERTED: Youth

36 KIND OF PEOPLE BECOMING CHURCH LEADERS: Young adults

37 QUALIFICATIONS OF PRESENT CHURCH LEADERSHIP:3-4 years training

38 MUSLIM INFLUENCE: (RATING SCALE 1 low - 5 very strong)
     POLITICS   ECONOMY   SOCIAL   RELIGION
39 DESIRABILITY TO BECOME A MUSLIM: WHICH SOCIAL GROUP:

SCRIPTURE

40 LITERATURE PUBLISHED IN VERNACULAR: DATE: IN PROCESS: None

41 CAN THEY READ SCRIPTURES IN ANOTHER LANGUAGE:

42 WHAT NEEDS EXIST THAT RELATE TO SCRIPTURES:

COMMENTS:

43. ATTITUDE TOWARD GOSPEL - 4

44. PRIORITY FOR ACTION - 2

IDENTIFICATION

   1 GROUP NAME: Glavda   2 POPULATION: 19,000 (SIL)

   3 STATE/DIVISION Gongola/Gwoza   4 ADMINISTRATIVE CENTRE : Gwoza

   5 LOCATION: East of Gwoza Hills S-Dghwede and Matakam E-Mandara

   6 DESCRIPTION: A Ethno-Long   B Rural   C Agric.

                  D Lower   E

   7 ACCESSIBILITY: Motor road, Trails, Semi-isolated

   8 COMMUNICATION MEDIA: Posta, Radio (Hospital)

   9 DYNAMICS OF UNIT: Growing, adopting new patterns

   10 INTERMARRIAGE: Yes accepted

   11 PART OF LARGER UNIT, NAME: RELATIONSHIP:

   12 POPULATION CENTRES / MARKET (M) / SCHOOL (S) Ngoshe M/S Cinine/Arboko Boko M/S

   13 FARM CROPS: G. corn, millet, beans, g. nuts

   14 MEDICAL FACILITIES: Hospital Ngoshe

LANGUAGE / LITERACY

   15 PRINCIPAL VERNACULAR: Glavda   16 TRADE LANGUAGE: Hausa   % USERS

   17 LITERATE ADULTS: 5 %   18 CHANGE IN LITERACY RATE: Decreasing

   19 PER CENT CHRISTIANS WHO ARE LITERATE: 80 %

   20 WHAT DO PEOPLE READ: Bible

   21 ESTIMATED ALJEMI READERS: None

RELIGIONS

   22 RELIGIOUS GROUPS: PER CENT OF UNIT: DECLINE/GROWTH:

      A. PROTESTANT (Christianity)   6   Rapid growth
      B. ROMAN CATHOLIC
      C. ISLAM   4   Slow growth
      D. ANIMIST   90   Declining
      E. INDEPENDENT CHURCHES

   23 PRESENT CHRISTIAN WITNESS: Yes Basel Mission EKAS GABAS

24 ORGANISED/UNORGANISED CHURCHES WITH ADHERENTS FROM THIS UNIT:

NAME	YEAR BEGUN	ADHERENTS	GROWTH TREND
EKAS GABAS	1965	500	Growing

25 ORGANISED CHURCHES WITH NO MEMBERS FROM THIS UNIT:

26 EARLIEST KNOWN CHRISTIAN WITNESS: GROUP: Basel Mission   YEAR: 1959

27 OPENNESS TO RELIGIOUS CHANGE: Open

28 PER CENT OF UNIT THAT HAS HEARD THE GOSPEL: 25-50 %

29 MOST EFFECTIVE METHODS USED: A.   Team Evang. 5 ·B. Evangelists living

30 MEDIA MOST ᵗᴴUSED BY: YOUTH   ADULTS   STUDENTS   OTHERS
   A. RADIO   x
   B. NEWSPAPER
   C.

31 FACTORS ENCOURAGING TO SPREAD OF CHRISTIANITY: Baptism of polygamists

32 FACTORS HINDERING SPREAD OF CHRISTIANITY: Muslim activity

33 ATTITUDE TOWARD CHRISTIANITY: Strongly favorable

34 AREA OF PRESENT CONCENTRATION: Whole tribe

35 KIND OF PEOPLE BEING CONVERTED: Adults, women, youth

36 KIND OF PEOPLE BECOMING CHURCH LEADERS: Kulu B.S. and T.C.N.N.

37 QUALIFICATIONS OF PRESENT CHURCH LEADERSHIP:

38 MUSLIM INFLUENCE: (RATING SCALE 1 low - 5 very strong)
     POLITICS 5   ECONOMY 3   SOCIAL 3 RELIGION 3

39 DESIRABILITY TO BECOME A MUSLIM: Yes   WHICH SOCIAL GROUP: Elders
                                                     Family Heads

SCRIPTURE

40 LITERATURE PUBLISHED IN VERNACULAR: DATE: IN PROCESS:
   Mark   1964

41 CAN THEY READ SCRIPTURES IN ANOTHER LANGUAGE: Hausa

42 WHAT NEEDS EXIST THAT RELATE TO SCRIPTURES: Scriptures not readily
     received   Hausa SC needed

COMMENTS:

   43.   ATTITUDE TOWARD GOSPEL - 4

   44.   PRIORITY FOR ACTION - 2

IDENTIFICATION

1 GROUP NAME: Dghwede (Jahode)   **2 POPULATION:** 13,000 (SIL)

3 STATE/DIVISION Gongola/Gwoza   **4 ADMINISTRATIVE CENTRE :** Gwoza

5 LOCATION: E-Cameroons W-Gwoza Hills N-Guduf S-Ndoshe

6 DESCRIPTION: A   B   C

          D   E

7 ACCESSIBILITY: Motor Road, Mountain trails

8 COMMUNICATION MEDIA: Postal - Gwoza

9 DYNAMICS OF UNIT: Growing, adopting new patterns/no change (SIL) '70

10 INTERMARRIAGE: Yes accepted

11 PART OF LARGER UNIT, NAME: **RELATIONSHIP:**

12 POPULATION CENTRES / MARKET (M) / SCHOOL (S) Barawa M/S '75
                                                 Wa'a (Ghwa'a, Jahode)

13 FARM CROPS: G corn, millett, beans

14 MEDICAL FACILITIES: First aid Barawa

LANGUAGE / LITERACY

15 PRINCIPAL VERNACULAR: Zighvana   **16 TRADE LANGUAGE:** Hausa   **% USERS**
                                                 Fulani   (Limited to few
17 LITERATE ADULTS: very **%** **18 CHANGE IN LITERACY RATE:** None
             few
19 PER CENT CHRISTIANS WHO ARE LITERATE: 5 **%**

20 WHAT DO PEOPLE READ: Bible

21 ESTIMATED ALJEMI READERS: None

RELIGIONS

22 RELIGIOUS GROUPS: **PER CENT OF UNIT:**   **DECLINE/GROWTH:**
    A. PROTESTANT   1%   Slow growth
    B. ROMAN CATHOLIC
    C. ISLAM
    D. ANIMIST   99%
    E. INDEPENDENT CHURCHES

23 PRESENT CHRISTIAN WITNESS: EKAS (Basel) EKAS Plateau

24 ORGANISED/UNORGANISED CHURCHES WITH ADHERENTS FROM THIS UNIT:

NAME	YEAR BEGUN	ADHERENTS	GROWTH TREND
EKAS/Basel Mission		35	

25 ORGANISED CHURCHES WITH NO MEMBERS FROM THIS UNIT:

26 EARLIEST KNOWN CHRISTIAN WITNESS: GROUP: Basel   YEAR: 1963

27 OPENNESS TO RELIGIOUS CHANGE: Slow

28 PER CENT OF UNIT THAT HAS HEARD THE GOSPEL: very few %

29 MOST EFFECTIVE METHODS USED: A. Visitation B. Teams 4

30 MEDIA MOST USED BY: YOUTH   ADULTS   STUDENTS   OTHERS

  A. Scriptures

  B.

  C.

31 FACTORS ENCOURAGING TO SPREAD OF CHRISTIANITY: Visitation Teams

32 FACTORS HINDERING SPREAD OF CHRISTIANITY: Beer drinking, Polygamy

33 ATTITUDE TOWARD CHRISTIANITY: Reluctant

34 AREA OF PRESENT CONCENTRATION: North

35 KIND OF PEOPLE BEING CONVERTED: Youth

36 KIND OF PEOPLE BECOMING CHURCH LEADERS: Youth

37 QUALIFICATIONS OF PRESENT CHURCH LEADERSHIP: 3 years training

38 MUSLIM INFLUENCE: (RATING SCALE 1 low - 5 very strong)

  POLITICS 1   ECONOMY   SOCIAL   RELIGION

39 DESIRABILITY TO BECOME A MUSLIM: no   WHICH SOCIAL GROUP:

SCRIPTURE

40 LITERATURE PUBLISHED IN VERNACULAR: DATE: IN PROCESS:
Portions unpublished (Begun 1971)
Mark, Primers in draft (1973)

41 CAN THEY READ SCRIPTURES IN ANOTHER LANGUAGE: No

42 WHAT NEEDS EXIST THAT RELATE TO SCRIPTURES: Literacy 8 children in
school 1975

COMMENTS:

43. ATTITUDE TOWARD GOSPEL - 3

44. PRIORITY FOR ACTION - 1

IDENTIFICATION

1 GROUP NAME: Fali   **2 POPULATION:** 25,000 (SIL)

3 STATE/DIVISION Gongola/Mubi   **4 ADMINISTRATIVE CENTRE :** Muchala

5 LOCATION: Mountains surrounding; Tribes, Margi Higi   Fulanis

6 DESCRIPTION: A Clan   **B** Sm. villages   **C** Towns

                D Scattered   **E**
                   farms

7 ACCESSIBILITY: Easily - road

8 COMMUNICATION MEDIA: Postal

9 DYNAMICS OF UNIT: Growing Stable Adopt new patterns

10 INTERMARRIAGE: Yes--accepted in and out

11 PART OF LARGER UNIT, NAME: Yes, Fali   **RELATIONSHIP:**

12 POPULATION CENTRES / MARKET (M) / SCHOOL (S) Muchala; Kirya; Mijlu;/Kirya (M);
Gazhiyam (M); Muchala (M); Muvur (M); Sahuda (M) Zhelivu (M);/ Vimtim (S) 1968
Sahuda (S); Mijilu (S); Kirya (S)

13 FARM CROPS: G. corn

14 MEDICAL FACILITIES: Dispensary--1

LANGUAGE / LITERACY

15 PRINCIPAL VERNACULAR: Fali   **16 TRADE LANGUAGE:** Hausa 50   **%** USERS
                                                Fulani 100

17 LITERATE ADULTS: **%** **18 CHANGE IN LITERACY RATE:**

19 PER CENT CHRISTIANS WHO ARE LITERATE: 3 **%**

20 WHAT DO PEOPLE READ: Bible (few)

21 ESTIMATED ALJEMI READERS:

RELIGIONS

22 RELIGIOUS GROUPS: **PER CENT OF UNIT:**   **DECLINE/GROWTH:**
   A. PROTESTANT   2%   Slow growth
   B. ROMAN CATHOLIC
   C. ISLAM   Stationary
   D. ANIMIST   95%   Slow growth
   E. INDEPENDENT CHURCHES   No

23 PRESENT CHRISTIAN WITNESS: Yes CBM

24 ORGANISED/UNORGANISED CHURCHES WITH ADHERENTS FROM THIS UNIT:

NAME	YEAR BEGUN	ADHERENTS	GROWTH TREND
CBM	1959	500	Growing

25 ORGANISED CHURCHES WITH NO MEMBERS FROM THIS UNIT: No

26 EARLIEST KNOWN CHRISTIAN WITNESS: GROUP: CBM   YEAR: 1959
                                              RCC, Baptist
27 OPENNESS TO RELIGIOUS CHANGE:

28 PER CENT OF UNIT THAT HAS HEARD THE GOSPEL: very few %

29 MOST EFFECTIVE METHODS USED: Preaching

30 MEDIA MOST USED BY:

	YOUTH	ADULTS	STUDENTS	OTHERS
A. RADIO	x		x	
B. NEWSPAPER				
C. SCRIPTURES	x	x	x	

31 FACTORS ENCOURAGING TO SPREAD OF CHRISTIANITY:

32 FACTORS HINDERING SPREAD OF CHRISTIANITY: Polygamy and drinking

33 ATTITUDE TOWARD CHRISTIANITY: Somewhat favorable

34 AREA OF PRESENT CONCENTRATION: North, South, West

35 KIND OF PEOPLE BEING CONVERTED: Youth, children

36 KIND OF PEOPLE BECOMING CHURCH LEADERS:

37 QUALIFICATIONS OF PRESENT CHURCH LEADERSHIP: Trained (1,2,3) years; untrained

38 MUSLIM INFLUENCE: (RATING SCALE 1 low - 5 very strong)
        POLITICS 5 ECONOMY 5 SOCIAL 5 RELIGION
39 DESIRABILITY TO BECOME A MUSLIM: Yes   WHICH SOCIAL GROUP: Family Heads

SCRIPTURE

40 LITERATURE PUBLISHED IN VERNACULAR: None DATE: IN PROCESS: None

41 CAN THEY READ SCRIPTURES IN ANOTHER LANGUAGE: Hausa

42 WHAT NEEDS EXIST THAT RELATE TO SCRIPTURES:

COMMENTS:

43. ATTITUDE TOWARD GOSPEL - 4

44. PRIORITY FOR ACTION - 1

IDENTIFICATION

1 GROUP NAME: Vere   2 POPULATION: 20,000

3 STATE/DIVISION Gongola/Adamawa   4 ADMINISTRATIVE CENTRE : Yola

5 LOCATION: Near Cameroon, Riv Bamwai, Mt. Kapkpaka, Bata, Chamba-S

6 DESCRIPTION: A Ethno-Ling   B Agri.   C Scattered farms

              D   E

7 ACCESSIBILITY: Isolated, road

8 COMMUNICATION MEDIA: Postal

9 DYNAMICS OF UNIT: Growing, resisting change

10 INTERMARRIAGE: Yes

11 PART OF LARGER UNIT, NAME: RELATIONSHIP:

12 POPULATION CENTRES / MARKET (M) / SCHOOL (S) Gurináti (S) Gurigwa
   Batti (M-S) Kurai, Karlahi (M-S) Yadim (M-S)

13 FARM CROPS: G nuts, millet, g. corn, rice

14 MEDICAL FACILITIES: First aid Gurinati / Dispensary Kerlahi

LANGUAGE / LITERACY

15 PRINCIPAL VERNACULAR: Vere   16 TRADE LANGUAGE: Fulani   90 % USERS

17 LITERATE ADULTS: %   18 CHANGE IN LITERACY RATE:

19 PER CENT CHRISTIANS WHO ARE LITERATE: 15 %

20 WHAT DO PEOPLE READ: Newspaper, Bible

21 ESTIMATED ALJEMI READERS: Few

RELIGIONS

22 RELIGIOUS GROUPS:	PER CENT OF UNIT:	DECLINE/GROWTH:
A. PROTESTANT	10%	Slow growth
B. ROMAN CATHOLIC	5%	Slow growth
C. ISLAM	5%	Slow growth
D. ANIMIST	80%	
E. INDEPENDENT CHURCHES	None	

23 PRESENT CHRISTIAN WITNESS: Lutheran church

24 ORGANISED/UNORGANISED CHURCHES WITH ADHERENTS FROM THIS UNIT:

NAME	YEAR BEGUN	ADHERENTS	GROWTH TREND
Lutheran	1950		

25 ORGANISED CHURCHES WITH NO MEMBERS FROM THIS UNIT:

26 EARLIEST KNOWN CHRISTIAN WITNESS: GROUP: Lutheran   YEAR:

27 OPENNESS TO RELIGIOUS CHANGE: Yes

28 PER CENT OF UNIT THAT HAS HEARD THE GOSPEL: 50-75 %

29 MOST EFFECTIVE METHODS USED:

30 MEDIA MOST USED BY:

	YOUTH	ADULTS	STUDENTS	OTHERS
A. RADIO		x	x	
B. NEWSPAPER				
C. BOOKS	X		X	

31 FACTORS ENCOURAGING TO SPREAD OF CHRISTIANITY: Drama, charts, radio, cinema, posters, preaching

32 FACTORS HINDERING SPREAD OF CHRISTIANITY: Preaching against polygamy & drinking

33 ATTITUDE TOWARD CHRISTIANITY: Strongly favorable

34 AREA OF PRESENT CONCENTRATION: North, south, west

35 KIND OF PEOPLE BEING CONVERTED: Adults, children

36 KIND OF PEOPLE BECOMING CHURCH LEADERS: Adults (Mature)

37 QUALIFICATIONS OF PRESENT CHURCH LEADERSHIP: Licensed

38 MUSLIM INFLUENCE: (RATING SCALE 1 low - 5 very strong)
POLITICS   ECONOMY 2 SOCIAL 2 RELIGION

39 DESIRABILITY TO BECOME A MUSLIM: Yes   WHICH SOCIAL GROUP: Family Heads Youth

SCRIPTURE

40 LITERATURE PUBLISHED IN VERNACULAR: None DATE: IN PROCESS:

41 CAN THEY READ SCRIPTURES IN ANOTHER LANGUAGE: Hausa

42 WHAT NEEDS EXIST THAT RELATE TO SCRIPTURES: Scripture in Vere & Fulfulde

COMMENTS:

43. ATTITUDE TOWARD GOSPEL - 4

44. PRIORITY FOR ACTION - 2

IDENTIFICATION

1 GROUP NAME: Mumuye   2 POPULATION: 200,000 (SIL)

3 STATE/DIVISION Gongola/Muri   4 ADMINISTRATIVE CENTRE :

5 LOCATION: MI S of Yola

6 DESCRIPTION: A Hamlets   B Agric.   C Ethno-Ling

                    D   E

7 ACCESSIBILITY: Those in hills difficult to reach

8 COMMUNICATION MEDIA: Radio   Postal

9 DYNAMICS OF UNIT: Growing, resisting change in remote areas

10 INTERMARRIAGE:

11 PART OF LARGER UNIT, NAME: RELATIONSHIP:

12 POPULATION CENTRES / MARKET (M) / SCHOOL (S)
    Zing Jalingo Panti Sawa

13 FARM CROPS:

14 MEDICAL FACILITIES:

LANGUAGE / LITERACY

15 PRINCIPAL VERNACULAR: Mumuye   16 TRADE LANGUAGE: Hausa   75 % USERS

17 LITERATE ADULTS: 5 %   18 CHANGE IN LITERACY RATE: Increasing

19 PER CENT CHRISTIANS WHO ARE LITERATE: 25 %

20 WHAT DO PEOPLE READ: Bible, newspaper

21 ESTIMATED ALJEMI READERS: Few

RELIGIONS

22 RELIGIOUS GROUPS:	PER CENT OF UNIT:	DECLINE/GROWTH:
A. PROTESTANT	-2%	Static
B. ROMAN CATHOLIC		
C. ISLAM	8-10%	Growing
D. ANIMIST	90%	Declining
E. INDEPENDENT CHURCHES		

23 PRESENT CHRISTIAN WITNESS: EKAS MURI (United Methodist)

24 ORGANISED/UNORGANISED CHURCHES WITH ADHERENTS FROM THIS UNIT:
   NAME   YEAR BEGUN   ADHERENTS   GROWTH TREND
   EKAS MURI   1954   Static
   Split in denomination caused stagnation

25 ORGANISED CHURCHES WITH NO MEMBERS FROM THIS UNIT:

26 EARLIEST KNOWN CHRISTIAN WITNESS: GROUP: YEAR:

27 OPENNESS TO RELIGIOUS CHANGE: Some

28 PER CENT OF UNIT THAT HAS HEARD THE GOSPEL: 25-50 %

29 MOST EFFECTIVE METHODS USED:

30 MEDIA MOST USED BY: YOUTH   ADULTS   STUDENTS   OTHERS
   A. RADIO   x   x
   B. NEWSPAPER
   C.

31 FACTORS ENCOURAGING TO SPREAD OF CHRISTIANITY: Church at Zing

32 FACTORS HINDERING SPREAD OF CHRISTIANITY: Churches split

33 ATTITUDE TOWARD CHRISTIANITY: Favorable

34 AREA OF PRESENT CONCENTRATION: North

35 KIND OF PEOPLE BEING CONVERTED:

36 KIND OF PEOPLE BECOMING CHURCH LEADERS:

37 QUALIFICATIONS OF PRESENT CHURCH LEADERSHIP: Bible School 3 years

38 MUSLIM INFLUENCE: (RATING SCALE 1 low - 5 very strong)
   POLITICS 4   ECONOMY 3   SOCIAL 3   RELIGION 3

39 DESIRABILITY TO BECOME A MUSLIM: 3   WHICH SOCIAL GROUP: Youth,
                                                         young adults

SCRIPTURE

40 LITERATURE PUBLISHED IN VERNACULAR: DATE: IN PROCESS:

41 CAN THEY READ SCRIPTURES IN ANOTHER LANGUAGE: Hausa

42 WHAT NEEDS EXIST THAT RELATE TO SCRIPTURES:

COMMENTS:

   43. ATTITUDE TOWARD GOSPEL - 3

   44. PRIORITY FOR ACTION - 2

IDENTIFICATION

1 GROUP NAME: DAKA (Dirim, Chamba)   **2 POPULATION:** 10,000

3 STATE/DIVISION Gongola/Mambilla,   **4 ADMINISTRATIVE CENTRE :** Ganye, Gembu
                        Southern
5 LOCATION: S.W. Taraba Riv/E.Cameroon/N. Chamba/ S. Jiru

6 DESCRIPTION: A Ethno-Ling   **B** Villages   **C** Agric.

                D Low   **E**

7 ACCESSIBILITY: Isolated Trails River

8 COMMUNICATION MEDIA: Few radios

9 DYNAMICS OF UNIT: Stable, resisting change

10 INTERMARRIAGE: Fulani Chambi Jibu

11 PART OF LARGER UNIT, NAME: Yes   **RELATIONSHIP:** Chambi

12 POPULATION CENTRES / MARKET (M) / SCHOOL (S)
    Gangumi M/S 1973

13 FARM CROPS: G. corn, maize, cotton, g. nuts

14 MEDICAL FACILITIES: Gangumi disp.

LANGUAGE / LITERACY

15 PRINCIPAL VERNACULAR: Dakanci   **16 TRADE LANGUAGE:** Fulfulde 30 **% USERS**
                                                        Hausa 20%
17 LITERATE ADULTS: 3 %   **18 CHANGE IN LITERACY RATE:**

19 PER CENT CHRISTIANS WHO ARE LITERATE: 50 %

20 WHAT DO PEOPLE READ: Bible

21 ESTIMATED ALJEMI READERS: Few

RELIGIONS

22 RELIGIOUS GROUPS: **PER CENT OF UNIT:**   **DECLINE/GROWTH:**
    A. PROTESTANT   2%   Slow growth
    B. ROMAN CATHOLIC   1%   Slow growth
    C. ISLAM   7-17%   Slow growth
    D. ANIMIST   80-90%   Declining
    E. INDEPENDENT CHURCHES

23 PRESENT CHRISTIAN WITNESS: EKAS Benue

24 ORGANISED/UNORGANISED CHURCHES WITH ADHERENTS FROM THIS UNIT:

NAME	YEAR BEGUN	ADHERENTS	GROWTH TREND
EKAS Benue	1970	40	

25 ORGANISED CHURCHES WITH NO MEMBERS FROM THIS UNIT:

26 EARLIEST KNOWN CHRISTIAN WITNESS: GROUP: SUM (CRC)   YEAR: 1960's

27 OPENNESS TO RELIGIOUS CHANGE: Slight but opening

28 PER CENT OF UNIT THAT HAS HEARD THE GOSPEL: very few 10%

29 MOST EFFECTIVE METHODS USED: A. Medical 3   B. House visit 4

30 MEDIA MOST USED BY: YOUTH   ADULTS   STUDENTS   OTHERS

	YOUTH	ADULTS	STUDENTS	OTHERS
A. RADIO		x		
B. NEWSPAPER				
C. SCRIPTURES		x		

31 FACTORS ENCOURAGING TO SPREAD OF CHRISTIANITY: Roads, Increased com-
                                                   munication
32 FACTORS HINDERING SPREAD OF CHRISTIANITY: Muslim ½emetratopm

33 ATTITUDE TOWARD CHRISTIANITY: Reluctant

34 AREA OF PRESENT CONCENTRATION: Lutheran North/EKAS South

35 KIND OF PEOPLE BEING CONVERTED: Youth

36 KIND OF PEOPLE BECOMING CHURCH LEADERS: Youth

37 QUALIFICATIONS OF PRESENT CHURCH LEADERSHIP: 4 in training Baissa

38 MUSLIM INFLUENCE: (RATING SCALE 1 low - 5 very strong)
     POLITICS 5   ECONOMY 5 SOCIAL 4   RELIGION 3
39 DESIRABILITY TO BECOME A MUSLIM: 3   WHICH SOCIAL GROUP: Youth
                                                    Family Head

SCRIPTURE

40 LITERATURE PUBLISHED IN VERNACULAR: DATE: IN PROCESS:
   No scriptures

41 CAN THEY READ SCRIPTURES IN ANOTHER LANGUAGE: Chamba, Hausa

42 WHAT NEEDS EXIST THAT RELATE TO SCRIPTURES: Study relationship of
                                               Chamba to Daka Low literacy

COMMENTS:

43. ATTITUDE TOWARD GOSPEL - 3

44. PRIORITY FOR ACTION - 1

IDENTIFICATION

1 GROUP NAME: Jibu   **2 POPULATION:** 20,000

3 STATE/DIVISION Gongola, Mambilla **4 ADMINISTRATIVE CENTRE :** Gembu, Jalingo
Muri

5 LOCATION: Taraba and Kam Rivers; Benue to Mambilla Plateau

6 DESCRIPTION: A Tribe   **B** Urban-small   **C** Scattered f-rms
villages
D Agric.   **E** Lower class; social and income

7 ACCESSIBILITY: Isolated; accessibile by trail, road, river, air

8 COMMUNICATION MEDIA: None

9 DYNAMICS OF UNIT: Stable, resisting change

10 INTERMARRIAGE: Yes, Hausa and Fulani

11 PART OF LARGER UNIT, NAME: Yes, Jukun   **RELATIONSHIP:** sub tribe

12 POPULATION CENTRES / MARKET (M) / SCHOOL (S) Gayam (M) Sun; Garbabi (S)
Hai Hula Sirti (11)-Fri Beli (M) Sat

13 FARM CROPS: G. corn, maize, rice cash crop

14 MEDICAL FACILITIES: Serti SUM Maternity: Beli: Garbabi: Jantari:
Serti Government Dispensaries

LANGUAGE / LITERACY

15 PRINCIPAL VERNACULAR: Jibu: Jibanci **16 TRADE LANGUAGE:** Fulani   **% USERS**
Hausa

17 LITERATE ADULTS: 3 %   **18 CHANGE IN LITERACY RATE:** Increasing

19 PER CENT CHRISTIANS WHO ARE LITERATE: 50 %

20 WHAT DO PEOPLE READ: Bible

21 ESTIMATED ALJEMI READERS: Few in towns

RELIGIONS

22 RELIGIOUS GROUPS: **PER CENT OF UNIT:**   **DECLINE/GROWTH:**
A. PROTESTANT   1%   Slow growth
B. ROMAN CATHOLIC
C. ISLAM
D. ANIMIST
E. INDEPENDENT CHURCHES

23 PRESENT CHRISTIAN WITNESS: Missionaries 12 (5 from Jibu) EKAS evangelists
and one pastor

24 ORGANISED/UNORGANISED CHURCHES WITH ADHERENTS FROM THIS UNIT:
<u>NAME</u>   <u>YEAR BEGUN</u>   <u>ADHERENTS</u>   <u>GROWTH TREND</u>

25 ORGANISED CHURCHES WITH NO MEMBERS FROM THIS UNIT: RCC

26 EARLIEST KNOWN CHRISTIAN WITNESS: GROUP: SUM CRC   **YEAR:** 1950

27 OPENNESS TO RELIGIOUS CHANGE:

28 PER CENT OF UNIT THAT HAS HEARD THE GOSPEL: very few 25%

29 MOST EFFECTIVE METHODS USED: A. House visitation (4) B. Gospel teams
                                                        C. Market preaching

30 MEDIA MOST USED BY: YOUTH   ADULTS   STUDENTS   OTHERS
    A. RADIO
    B. NEWSPAPER
    C.

31 FACTORS ENCOURAGING TO SPREAD OF CHRISTIANITY: Communications and
                                                                 road
32 FACTORS HINDERING SPREAD OF CHRISTIANITY: Islam

33 ATTITUDE TOWARD CHRISTIANITY: Reluctant

34 AREA OF PRESENT CONCENTRATION:

35 KIND OF PEOPLE BEING CONVERTED: Youth

36 KIND OF PEOPLE BECOMING CHURCH LEADERS: Young men

37 QUALIFICATIONS OF PRESENT CHURCH LEADERSHIP: Trained 4 years

38 MUSLIM INFLUENCE: (RATING SCALE 1 low - 5 **very strong**)
    POLITICS   ECONOMY 5   SOCIAL 3   RELIGION
39 DESIRABILITY TO BECOME A MUSLIM: WHICH SOCIAL GROUP: Elders

SCRIPTURE

    40 LITERATURE PUBLISHED IN VERNACULAR: DATE: IN PROCESS:
        Gospels 1973   New Testament

    41 CAN THEY READ SCRIPTURES IN ANOTHER LANGUAGE: Hausa

    42 WHAT NEEDS EXIST THAT RELATE TO SCRIPTURES: Literacy

COMMENTS:

    43. ATTITUDE TOWARD GOSPEL - 3

    44. PRIORITY FOR ACTION - 2

IDENTIFICATION

1 GROUP NAME: Ndoro   2 POPULATION: 10,000

3 STATE/DIVISION Gongola Mambilla   4 ADMINISTRATIVE CENTRE : Gembu

5 LOCATION: N and E Jibu S-Cameroon W-Tiv

6 DESCRIPTION: A Agric.   B Villages   C

                       D   E

7 ACCESSIBILITY: Semi isolated road trails

8 COMMUNICATION MEDIA:

9 DYNAMICS OF UNIT:

10 INTERMARRIAGE:

11 PART OF LARGER UNIT, NAME: RELATIONSHIP:

12 POPULATION CENTRES / MARKET (M) / SCHOOL (S)
   Baissa Ndafor

13 FARM CROPS:

14 MEDICAL FACILITIES:

LANGUAGE / LITERACY

15 PRINCIPAL VERNACULAR: Ndoro   16 TRADE LANGUAGE: Hausa   75 % USERS

17 LITERATE ADULTS: 5 %   18 CHANGE IN LITERACY RATE: Increasing

19 PER CENT CHRISTIANS WHO ARE LITERATE: 25% ?

20 WHAT DO PEOPLE READ:

21 ESTIMATED ALJEMI READERS:

RELIGIONS

22 RELIGIOUS GROUPS: PER CENT OF UNIT: DECLINE/GROWTH:
   A. PROTESTANT   5-10%
   B. ROMAN CATHOLIC
   C. ISLAM
   D. ANIMIST   90-95%   Decline
   E. INDEPENDENT CHURCHES
23 PRESENT CHRISTIAN WITNESS: EKAS Benue

24 ORGANISED/UNORGANISED CHURCHES WITH ADHERENTS FROM THIS UNIT:
   NAME   YEAR BEGUN   ADHERENTS   GROWTH TREND
   EKAS Benue (Baissa)
   2 churches 10 preaching points

25 ORGANISED CHURCHES WITH NO MEMBERS FROM THIS UNIT:

26 EARLIEST KNOWN CHRISTIAN WITNESS: GROUP: S.U.M.   YEAR:

27 OPENNESS TO RELIGIOUS CHANGE: Moderate

28 PER CENT OF UNIT THAT HAS HEARD THE GOSPEL: %

29 MOST EFFECTIVE METHODS USED:

30 MEDIA MOST USED BY: YOUTH   ADULTS   STUDENTS   OTHERS
   A. RADIO
   B. NEWSPAPER
   C.

31 FACTORS ENCOURAGING TO SPREAD OF CHRISTIANITY: Bible School at Baissa

32 FACTORS HINDERING SPREAD OF CHRISTIANITY: Cultural upheaval

33 ATTITUDE TOWARD CHRISTIANITY: Favorable

34 AREA OF PRESENT CONCENTRATION:

35 KIND OF PEOPLE BEING CONVERTED: Youth Young adults

36 KIND OF PEOPLE BECOMING CHURCH LEADERS:

37 QUALIFICATIONS OF PRESENT CHURCH LEADERSHIP: Bible School

38 MUSLIM INFLUENCE: (RATING SCALE 1 low - 5 very strong)
   POLITICS 2   ECONOMY   SOCIAL   RELIGION 2
39 DESIRABILITY TO BECOME A MUSLIM: 2   WHICH SOCIAL GROUP:

SCRIPTURE
   40 LITERATURE PUBLISHED IN VERNACULAR: DATE: IN PROCESS:
                    None

   41 CAN THEY READ SCRIPTURES IN ANOTHER LANGUAGE: Hausa

   42 WHAT NEEDS EXIST THAT RELATE TO SCRIPTURES:

COMMENTS:

   43. ATTITUDE TOWARD GOSPEL - 3-4

   44. PRIORITY FOR .ACTION - 2

IDENTIFICATION

1 GROUP NAME: Kambari   **2 POPULATION:** 100,000

3 STATE/DIVISION Niger/Kontagora   **4 ADMINISTRATIVE CENTRE:** Kontagora

5 LOCATION: N of Kontagora /Dakarkari-N/ Kamuru - E / Niger Riv - W.

6 DESCRIPTION: A Ethno-Ling   **B** Villages   **C** Agric.

                D   **E**

7 ACCESSIBILITY: Semi isolated   road   river

8 COMMUNICATION MEDIA: Postal   road

9 DYNAMICS OF UNIT: Growing/adopting new patterns/some resistance

10 INTERMARRIAGE: No

11 PART OF LARGER UNIT, NAME: No   **RELATIONSHIP:**

12 POPULATION CENTRES / MARKET (M) / SCHOOL (S) Kontagora, Salka M-Sat/S, Auna M-Th/S, Makuku S, Ibeto M-Fr/S, Agwara S

13 FARM CROPS: G. nuts, maize, g. corn, cotton

14 MEDICAL FACILITIES: Dispensaries

LANGUAGE / LITERACY

15 PRINCIPAL VERNACULAR: Kambarci   **16 TRADE LANGUAGE:** Hausa   75 **% USERS**

17 LITERATE ADULTS: 15 %   **18 CHANGE IN LITERACY RATE:**

19 PER CENT CHRISTIANS WHO ARE LITERATE: 25 %

20 WHAT DO PEOPLE READ: Gaskiya books, Bible

21 ESTIMATED ALJEMI READERS: A few in towns

RELIGIONS

22 RELIGIOUS GROUPS:	**PER CENT OF UNIT:**	**DECLINE/GROWTH:**
A. PROTESTANT	5	Slow growth
B. ROMAN CATHOLIC	5	Static
C. ISLAM	25	Slow growth
D. ANIMIST	65	Declining
E. INDEPENDENT CHURCHES		

23 PRESENT CHRISTIAN WITNESS: UMCA Baptist

24 ORGANISED/UNORGANISED CHURCHES WITH ADHERENTS FROM THIS UNIT:

NAME	YEAR BEGUN	ADHERENTS	GROWTH TREND
UMCA	1935		
Baptist	1950		

25 ORGANISED CHURCHES WITH NO MEMBERS FROM THIS UNIT:

26 EARLIEST KNOWN CHRISTIAN WITNESS: GROUP: U.M.C.   YEAR: 1935

27 OPENNESS TO RELIGIOUS CHANGE: Very favorable

28 PER CENT OF UNIT THAT HAS HEARD THE GOSPEL: 10-25 %

29 MOST EFFECTIVE METHODS USED: House visit.

30 MEDIA MOST USED BY:

	YOUTH	ADULTS	STUDENTS	OTHERS
A. RADIO	x	x	x	
B. SCRIPTURES			x	
C. GENERAL LITERATURE		X		

31 FACTORS ENCOURAGING TO SPREAD OF CHRISTIANITY: Records in Kambari Tape and record players

32 FACTORS HINDERING SPREAD OF CHRISTIANITY:

33 ATTITUDE TOWARD CHRISTIANITY: Somewhat favorable   Somewhat hostile

34 AREA OF PRESENT CONCENTRATION: North

35 KIND OF PEOPLE BEING CONVERTED: All ages

36 KIND OF PEOPLE BECOMING CHURCH LEADERS: Mature adults

37 QUALIFICATIONS OF PRESENT CHURCH LEADERSHIP: Licensed 4 years traing

38 MUSLIM INFLUENCE: (RATING SCALE 1 low - 5 very strong)
POLITICS 2   ECONOMY 2 SOCIAL 2 RELIGION 2

39 DESIRABILITY TO BECOME A MUSLIM: Yes   WHICH SOCIAL GROUP: Youth

SCRIPTURE

40 LITERATURE PUBLISHED IN VERNACULAR: None DATE: IN PROCESS: None

41 CAN THEY READ SCRIPTURES IN ANOTHER LANGUAGE: Hausa

42 WHAT NEEDS EXIST THAT RELATE TO SCRIPTURES: Kambari translation greatly needed - no Scripture in Kambarci

COMMENTS:

43. ATTITUDE TOWARD GOSPEL - 3-4

44. PRIORITY FOR ACTION - 1

IDENTIFICATION

   1 GROUP NAME: Duka   **2 POPULATION:** 10,000

   3 STATE/DIVISION Niger/Kontagora   **4 ADMINISTRATIVE CENTRE :** Rijau

   5 LOCATION: T. Magajiya/Dakarkari-N/ Kambari - S & W

   6 DESCRIPTION: A   **B**   **C**

                      D   **E**

   7 ACCESSIBILITY: Semi isolated road trails

   8 COMMUNICATION MEDIA: Postal radio

   9 DYNAMICS OF UNIT: Stable growing

   10 INTERMARRIAGE:

   11 PART OF LARGER UNIT, NAME: **RELATIONSHIP:**

   12 POPULATION CENTRES / **MARKET (M)** / **SCHOOL (S)**
        T. Magajiya (M) (S) Hosp.

   13 FARM CROPS:

   14 MEDICAL FACILITIES: Hospital

LANGUAGE / LITERACY

   15 PRINCIPAL VERNACULAR: Dukanci   **16 TRADE LANGUAGE:** Hausa   95 **%** USERS

   17 LITERATE ADULTS: 2 **%** **18 CHANGE IN LITERACY RATE:** None

   19 PER CENT CHRISTIANS WHO ARE LITERATE: **%**

   20 WHAT DO PEOPLE READ:

   21 ESTIMATED ALJEMI READERS: Few only

RELIGIONS

   22 RELIGIOUS GROUPS: **PER CENT OF UNIT:**   **DECLINE/GROWTH:**
       A. PROTESTANT   -1%
       B. ROMAN CATHOLIC
       C. ISLAM   10%
       D. ANIMIST   90%
       E. INDEPENDENT CHURCHES

   23 PRESENT CHRISTIAN WITNESS:

24 ORGANISED/UNORGANISED CHURCHES WITH ADHERENTS FROM THIS UNIT:
   <u>NAME</u>   <u>YEAR BEGUN</u>   <u>ADHERENTS</u>   <u>GROWTH TREND</u>
   UMCA   25-50   Slow growth

25 ORGANISED CHURCHES WITH NO MEMBERS FROM THIS UNIT:

26 EARLIEST KNOWN CHRISTIAN WITNESS: GROUP: YEAR:

27 OPENNESS TO RELIGIOUS CHANGE: Favorable

28 PER CENT OF UNIT THAT HAS HEARD THE GOSPEL: 25-50 %

29 MOST EFFECTIVE METHODS USED:

30 MEDIA MOST USED BY: YOUTH   ADULTS   STUDENTS   OTHERS
   A. RADIO   x   x   x
   B. NEWSPAPER
   C.

31 FACTORS ENCOURAGING TO SPREAD OF CHRISTIANITY: Strong church in T. Magajiya, mostly Dakarkari who could help to evangelize

32 FACTORS HINDERING SPREAD OF CHRISTIANITY: Need for trained Dukawa
                                             evangelists
33 ATTITUDE TOWARD CHRISTIANITY: Very favorable

34 AREA OF PRESENT CONCENTRATION:

35 KIND OF PEOPLE BEING CONVERTED: Youth

36 KIND OF PEOPLE BECOMING CHURCH LEADERS:

37 QUALIFICATIONS OF PRESENT CHURCH LEADERSHIP:

38 MUSLIM INFLUENCE: (RATING SCALE 1 low - 5 very strong)
   POLITICS 2   ECONOMY 2 SOCIAL 2   RELIGION 2
39 DESIRABILITY TO BECOME A MUSLIM: 2   WHICH SOCIAL GROUP:Youth

<u>SCRIPTURE</u>

40 LITERATURE PUBLISHED IN VERNACULAR: DATE: IN PROCESS:
   2 UMS missionaries doing translation and literacy

41 CAN THEY READ SCRIPTURES IN ANOTHER LANGUAGE: Hausa

42 WHAT NEEDS EXIST THAT RELATE TO SCRIPTURES: Stronger motivation Lack of
                                                                  interest

<u>COMMENTS:</u>

   43. ATTITUDE TOWARD GOSPEL - 4

   44. PRIORITY FOR ACTION - 2

IDENTIFICATION

1 GROUP NAME: Faka   2 POPULATION: 15,000 (SIL)

3 STATE/DIVISION Niger/Kontagora   4 ADMINISTRATIVE CENTRE : Zuru

5 LOCATION: Dukawa-S / Dakarkari-E / Hausa-N & W / NW of Rijau

6 DESCRIPTION: A Ethno-Ling   B Agric.   C Villages

                D   E

7 ACCESSIBILITY: Semi isolated Road trails

8 COMMUNICATION MEDIA:

9 DYNAMICS OF UNIT:

10 INTERMARRIAGE:

11 PART OF LARGER UNIT, NAME: RELATIONSHIP:

12 POPULATION CENTRES / MARKET (M) / SCHOOL (S)   No Fakawa in secondary, 2 RCC
Schools, 2 N.A. Schools

13 FARM CROPS: G. corn, millet, maize, beans, rice, cassava, yams

14 MEDICAL FACILITIES:

LANGUAGE / LITERACY

15 PRINCIPAL VERNACULAR: Faka   16 TRADE LANGUAGE: 60-70 % USERS

17 LITERATE ADULTS: few %   18 CHANGE IN LITERACY RATE: Very slow increase

19 PER CENT CHRISTIANS WHO ARE LITERATE: %

20 WHAT DO PEOPLE READ:

21 ESTIMATED ALJEMI READERS:

RELIGIONS

22 RELIGIOUS GROUPS: PER CENT OF UNIT: DECLINE/GROWTH:
   A. PROTESTANT   -1
   B. ROMAN CATHOLIC   -1   Losing ground
   C. ISLAM   15   Slow growth
   D. ANIMIST   85   Declining
   E. INDEPENDENT CHURCHES
23 PRESENT CHRISTIAN WITNESS: UMCA 2 churches

24 ORGANISED/UNORGANISED CHURCHES WITH ADHERENTS FROM THIS UNIT:

NAME	YEAR BEGUN	ADHERENTS	GROWTH TREND
UMCA		40	Slow

25 ORGANISED CHURCHES WITH NO MEMBERS FROM THIS UNIT:

26 EARLIEST KNOWN CHRISTIAN WITNESS: GROUP: U.M.S.   YEAR:

27 OPENNESS TO RELIGIOUS CHANGE: Some

28 PER CENT OF UNIT THAT HAS HEARD THE GOSPEL: 25 %

29 MOST EFFECTIVE METHODS USED:

30 MEDIA MOST USED BY: YOUTH   ADULTS   STUDENTS   OTHERS
   A. RADIO
   B. NEWSPAPER
   C.

31 FACTORS ENCOURAGING TO SPREAD OF CHRISTIANITY: Dakarkari believers are
                                                  evangelizing
32 FACTORS HINDERING SPREAD OF CHRISTIANITY:
                                R.C.C. influence
33 ATTITUDE TOWARD CHRISTIANITY:
                        Favorable
34 AREA OF PRESENT CONCENTRATION:

35 KIND OF PEOPLE BEING CONVERTED:

36 KIND OF PEOPLE BECOMING CHURCH LEADERS:

37 QUALIFICATIONS OF PRESENT CHURCH LEADERSHIP:

38 MUSLIM INFLUENCE: (RATING SCALE 1 low - 5 very strong)
   POLITICS ^{3} ECONOMY ^{3} SOCIAL ^{2} RELIGION ^{2}

39 DESIRABILITY TO BECOME A MUSLIM: 2   WHICH SOCIAL GROUP:

SCRIPTURE

40 LITERATURE PUBLISHED IN VERNACULAR: DATE: IN PROCESS:
                             Nil

41 CAN THEY READ SCRIPTURES IN ANOTHER LANGUAGE: Hausa

42 WHAT NEEDS EXIST THAT RELATE TO SCRIPTURES:

COMMENTS:

43. ATTITUDE TOWARD GOSPEL - 3-4

44. PRIORITYFOR ACTION - 2

IDENTIFICATION

1 GROUP NAME: Gbari Yamma   **2 POPULATION:** 100,000

3 STATE/DIVISION Niger/Minna   **4 ADMINISTRATIVE CENTRE :** Minna

5 LOCATION: Nupes-S Koro Kadara-E/ Kamuku-W

6 DESCRIPTION: A Ethno-Ling **B** Agric. **C** Villages

                  D   **E**

7 ACCESSIBILITY: Remote

8 COMMUNICATION MEDIA: Stable, slow to chang e

9 DYNAMICS OF UNIT: Increasing

10 INTERMARRIAGE: W. Hausa

11 PART OF LARGER UNIT, NAME: Gbari Matai   **RELATIONSHIP:**

12 POPULATION CENTRES / MARKET (M) / SCHOOL (S)
Minna M S, Paiko M S

13 FARM CROPS: G. corn, millet, maize, g nuts, rice, sugar cane

14 MEDICAL FACILITIES: Hospital clinics

LANGUAGE / LITERACY

15 PRINCIPAL VERNACULAR: Gbari   **16 TRADE LANGUAGE:** Hausa   75 **% USERS**

17 LITERATE ADULTS: **%**   **18 CHANGE IN LITERACY RATE:**

19 PER CENT CHRISTIANS WHO ARE LITERATE: **%**

20 WHAT DO PEOPLE READ:

21 ESTIMATED ALJEMI READERS: A few in towns

RELIGIONS

22 RELIGIOUS GROUPS:	PER CENT OF UNIT:	DECLINE/GROWTH:
A. PROTESTANT	-5%	Very slow growth
B. ROMAN CATHOLIC	-5%	Very slow growth
C. ISLAM	20%	Growing
D. ANIMIST	75%	
E. INDEPENDENT CHURCHES		

23 PRESENT CHRISTIAN WITNESS: ECWA   Baptist

24 ORGANISED/UNORGANISED CHURCHES WITH ADHERENTS FROM THIS UNIT:

NAME	YEAR BEGUN	ADHERENTS	GROWTH TREND
ECWA (SIM)	1930		Slow
Baptist	1950		Slow

25 ORGANISED CHURCHES WITH NO MEMBERS FROM THIS UNIT:

26 EARLIEST KNOWN CHRISTIAN WITNESS: GROUP: S.I.M.   YEAR: 1910

27 OPENNESS TO RELIGIOUS CHANGE: Reluctant

28 PER CENT OF UNIT THAT HAS HEARD THE GOSPEL: 25-50 %

29 MOST EFFECTIVE METHODS USED: A. Preaching B. Visit C. Market open air

30 MEDIA MOST USED BY:

	YOUTH	ADULTS	STUDENTS	OTHERS
A. RADIO	x	x	x	
B. NEWSPAPER				
C. GASKIYA BOOKS	x		x	

31 FACTORS ENCOURAGING TO SPREAD OF CHRISTIANITY: Nearby Matai could evangelize these

32 FACTORS HINDERING SPREAD OF CHRISTIANITY: Comity among mission/churches

33 ATTITUDE TOWARD CHRISTIANITY: Unfavorable, resistant

34 AREA OF PRESENT CONCENTRATION: Around Minna

35 KIND OF PEOPLE BEING CONVERTED: Youth

36 KIND OF PEOPLE BECOMING CHURCH LEADERS: Young adults

37 QUALIFICATIONS OF PRESENT CHURCH LEADERSHIP: 3-4 years training

38 MUSLIM INFLUENCE: (RATING SCALE 1 low - 5 very strong)
    POLITICS 4   ECONOMY 3   SOCIAL 4   RELIGION 4

39 DESIRABILITY TO BECOME A MUSLIM: 4   WHICH SOCIAL GROUP: Young adults

SCRIPTURE

40 LITERATURE PUBLISHED IN VERNACULAR: DATE: IN PROCESS:
   N.T.   1956 but not popular, Hausa preferred

41 CAN THEY READ SCRIPTURES IN ANOTHER LANGUAGE: Hausa

42 WHAT NEEDS EXIST THAT RELATE TO SCRIPTURES:
   Teach literacy-lack of interest in it

COMMENTS:

43. ATTITUDE TOWARD GOSPEL - 2

44. PRIORITY FOR ACTION - 2

IDENTIFICATION

1 GROUP NAME: Kamuku   **2 POPULATION:** 20,000

3 STATE/DIVISION Niger/Minna   **4 ADMINISTRATIVE CENTRE :** Minna

5 LOCATION: NW of Minna/Gbari on SE/Kambari W / Hausa N

6 DESCRIPTION: A Villages   **B** Agric.   **C** Ethno Ling

            D   **E**

7 ACCESSIBILITY: Semi isolated trail road

8 COMMUNICATION MEDIA: Postal radio

9 DYNAMICS OF UNIT: Stable, adopting new patterns

10 INTERMARRIAGE: No (with exceptions)

11 PART OF LARGER UNIT, NAME: **RELATIONSHIP:**

12 POPULATION CENTRES / MARKET (M) / SCHOOL (S) Tungan Bako M-M S, Mariga M-Sat.S
Kagara M-Tu/SS, Pandogari M-Sat.S., Markujeri M-Th S., Tegina M-Fr. S.,
Kwana M-Wed., Kimbi M-Wed.

13 FARM CROPS: G. corn, millet, yams, g. nuts

14 MEDICAL FACILITIES:

LANGUAGE / LITERACY

15 PRINCIPAL VERNACULAR: Kamuku   **16 TRADE LANGUAGE:** Hausa   100% USERS

17 LITERATE ADULTS: 10 %   **18 CHANGE IN LITERACY RATE:** Increasing

19 PER CENT CHRISTIANS WHO ARE LITERATE: +50%

20 WHAT DO PEOPLE READ: Gaskiya books, Bible

21 ESTIMATED ALJEMI READERS:

RELIGIONS

22 RELIGIOUS GROUPS:	PER CENT OF UNIT:	DECLINE/GROWTH:
A. PROTESTANT	5	Slow growth
B. ROMAN CATHOLIC		
C. ISLAM	20	Slow growth
D. ANIMIST	75	Declining
E. INDEPENDENT CHURCHES	none	

23 PRESENT CHRISTIAN WITNESS: ECWA   Baptist

24 ORGANISED/UNORGANISED CHURCHES WITH ADHERENTS FROM THIS UNIT:

NAME	YEAR BEGUN	ADHERENTS	GROWTH TREND
Baptist	1959	400	Growing slowly
ECWA	1960	150	Growing slowly

25 ORGANISED CHURCHES WITH NO MEMBERS FROM THIS UNIT:

26 EARLIEST KNOWN CHRISTIAN WITNESS: GROUP: Tuller   YEAR: 1940

27 OPENNESS TO RELIGIOUS CHANGE: Yes. Several Baptist preaching
                                 stations in last 10 years

28 PER CENT OF UNIT THAT HAS HEARD THE GOSPEL: 25-50 %

29 MOST EFFECTIVE METHODS USED: A. Preaching stations B. C.R.I. - schools
                                C. Visitation

30 MEDIA MOST USED BY: YOUTH   ADULTS   STUDENTS   OTHERS

   A. RADIO

   B. NEWSPAPER

   C.

31 FACTORS ENCOURAGING TO SPREAD OF CHRISTIANITY: Consistent visitation by
missionaries, national and expatriate

32 FACTORS HINDERING SPREAD OF CHRISTIANITY: Pressure of Muslim leaders

33 ATTITUDE TOWARD CHRISTIANITY: Somewhat favorable

34 AREA OF PRESENT CONCENTRATION:

35 KIND OF PEOPLE BEING CONVERTED: Youth

36 KIND OF PEOPLE BECOMING CHURCH LEADERS: Young adults

37 QUALIFICATIONS OF PRESENT CHURCH LEADERSHIP: 4 years training

38 MUSLIM INFLUENCE: (RATING SCALE 1 low - 5 very strong)
   POLITICS ^{5} ECONOMY ^{4} SOCIAL ^{3} RELIGION ^{4}

39 DESIRABILITY TO BECOME A MUSLIM: Yes   WHICH SOCIAL GROUP: Village Heads

SCRIPTURE

  40 LITERATURE PUBLISHED IN VERNACULAR: DATE: IN PROCESS:

  41 CAN THEY READ SCRIPTURES IN ANOTHER LANGUAGE: Hausa (widely used)

  42 WHAT NEEDS EXIST THAT RELATE TO SCRIPTURES:

    No scripture in process   Illiteracy

COMMENTS:

43. ATTITUDE TOWARD GOSPEL - 2-3

44. PRIORITY FOR ACTION - 1

B.
Cultural Commonalities

Chart of Common Cultural Characteristics
Having Specific Effect on Church Planting

Key to Chart

```
x=Yes      U=Unevangelized
0=No       P=Partially Ev.
?=Unknown  R=Resistant
1-5=Level of intensity
       low 1  3  5 high
```

TRADITIONAL RELIGION

1. high god
2. lesser gods
3. priests
4. sacred groves, mountains
5. tabus: animals, foods
6. blood sacrifices
7. other sacrifices
8. fetishes
9. rebirth
10. sorcery causes death

Region	Language	Status	1	2	3	4	5	6	7	8	9	10
North West	Kamuku	P	x	x	x	x	x	x	x	x	x	x
North West	Gbari Yamma	P	x	x	x	x	x	x	4	x	x	x
North West	Fakai	P	x	x	x	?	x	x	x	x	x	x
North West	Duka	P	x	x	x	x	x	4	x	x	x	x
North West	Kambari	P	x	4	x	x	4	4	4	4	x	x
North East	Ndoro	P	x	x	x	5	5	x	x	x	x	x
North East	Jibu	P	x	x	x	5	5	4	x	x	x	x
North East	Daka	U	x	x	x	5	4	4	x	x	x	x
North East	Mumuye	P	x	x	x	x	x	x	x	x	x	x
North East	Vere	P	x	x	x	x	x	4	x	x	x	x
North East	Fali	P	x	4	3	x	4	4	4	x	x	x
North East	* Mandara Mtn.	P	x	4	x	4	4	4	4	x	?	x
North East	Ngamo	P	x	x	x	?	4	4	x	x	x	0
North East	Babir Thali	U	x	x	x	?	2	x	2	3	x	x
North East	# Zaranda Hill	U	x	x	x	x	x	x	x	x	x	?
North East	Jarawa	P	x	x	x	x	x	x	x	x	x	x
North East	Miya	P	x	4	x	x	x	x	x	x	x	x
North East	Warji	R	x	4	x	x	x	x	x	x	x	x
North East	Butawa	U	x	x	x	x	4	4	x	x	x	?
North East	Afawa	U	x	x	x	x	x	x	x	x	x	?
North Central	Koro	P	x	x	x	x	x	x	x	x	x	x
North Central	Kadara	P	x	2	3	x	x	x	x	x	x	?
North Central	Hausa Maguzawa	P	x	2	3	0	0	x	x	x	x	?
Kwara	Igbirra	R	x	3	4	x	4	4	4	x	x	?
Kwara	Bussa	P	x	3	x	x	4	4	4	x	x	?
Benue Plateau	Gwandara	U	x	4	4	4	5	4	4	5	x	x
Benue Plateau	Gade	P	4	4	4	3	4	4	4	4	x	x
Benue Plateau	Bassa	P	x	4	x	x	4	4	4	4	x	x
Benue Plateau	Afo	P	x	5	2	x	4	3	5	5	?	x
Benue Plateau	Alago	P	x	4	2	3	4	3	4	4	?	x

FAMILY
11. extended family
12. trad. betrothal
13. marriage: exogamous
14.   exchange
15.   levirate
16.   dowry
17.   polygamy
18. ancestor veneration

OCCUPATIONS
19. agriculture
20. fishing, hunting
21. crafts

EDUCATION
22. informal, example
23. formal, western

COMMUNITY
24. leaders' influence
    group influence
    readiness to change

FAMILY																		
11. extended family	x	x	x	x	x	x	x	x	x	x	x	x	2	x	x	x	x	x
12. trad. betrothal	3	3	3	x	x	x	4	x	3	?	?	?	x	x	x	x	x	3
13. marriage: exogamous	x	x	x	o	x	x	x	o	o	o	o	o	o	x	x	x	o	x
14. exchange	o	x	x	o	o	o	o	o	?	?	?	?	o	x	x	x	o	o
15. levirate	x	x	x	o	?	x	?	?	x	x	x	x	x	x	x	x	o	x
16. dowry	3	x	x	x	1	x	x	x	2	1	x	x	2	x	x	x	x	x
17. polygamy	3	4	3	x	x	x	x	2	x	x	x	5	x	2	2	2	2	x
18. ancestor veneration	5	5	5	4	4	4	5	4	4	1	x	4	4	x	x	4	4	5
OCCUPATIONS																		
19. agriculture	5	5	5	5	5	5	5	5	5	5	5	5	5	5	5	5	5	5
20. fishing, hunting	3	3	3	2	2	3	3	3	3	x	x	3	4	4	x	3	x	4
21. crafts	3	x	3	3	4	x	3	3	x	3	x	3	x	3	x	x	x	x
EDUCATION																		
22. informal, example	x	x	x	x	x	x	x	x	x	x	x	x	x	x	x	x	x	x
23. formal, western	1	1	1	1	3	3	2	1	1	2	1	1	2	3	1	2	3	2
COMMUNITY																		
24. leaders' influence	4	4	3	4	4	4	4	4	4	4	5	2	2	5	4	5	4	5
group influence	4	4	4	4	4	5	4	4	4	4	5	2	2	5	4	5	4	4
readiness to change	3	3	4	2	3	4	3	3	2	4	3	2	3	3	2	3	4	2

\# Zaranda Hill = Geji, Zul, Bolu, Pelu, Girma

* Mandara Mtn. = Zhaladivha, Hidkala, Dghwede, Guduf, Glavda, Ngoshe, Sukur, Tur, Vemgo

C.

Sample Lesson Series

(For Use in Systematic Village Evangelism)

Purpose and Intent of These Lessons

a. To provide a set of Bible stories for village evangelism.
b. To use the story to present vital teaching about God, man, sin, salvation.
c. To enable people to understand man's relations to God and his need for a Saviour.
d. To lead them naturally to the story of Jesus Christ.
e. To encourage a group to make a decision for Christ.

How to Use These Stories

a. Read the account of the story in the Bible carefully until you understand it thoroughly.
b. Practise telling the story in your own words to your family or friends. Tell it as though you just saw it happen yesterday.
c. Select the main teaching that you will emphasize. How can you do this without preaching? You must do it by just telling the story.
d. Discussion after the story. Prepare the questions that will help you begin the discussion. Emphasize the main teaching again.

e. Arrange with some friendly people to meet with you each week.

f. Usually tell a new story each week. YOu may want to review the last one. Or you may find it best to tell the same one again.
g. Listen to their questions to see if they are understanding you.
h. Be patient about asking for a decision to follow Christ. Don't be in a hurry. The jailer said, "What must I do to be saved?" Wait until a number are ready and then draw the net towards the end of these lessons.

Other Suggestions

a. You need to aim your teaching at adults. Do not become a "Children's teacher" at this point. Arrange with them as to the best time for gathering.
b. Always read several important verses from God's Word.
c. A simple song with an African tune may be helpful.

Story and Bible Reference	*Main Teaching to be Emphasized*
Creation Gen. 1 - 2.	God created the world, man, animals 2:7. Man is responsible to God 1:27
Man disobeyed God Gen. 2:15-17; 3:1-19.	Man disobeyed God and hid from Him. God looked for man and found him.
The first sacrifice Gen. 3:15-24.	Sacrifice of an animal for sin. Man will now die. Wages of sin is death Rom. 6:23.
Cain kills Abel Gen. 4.	Evil increases. God's way is to sacrifice an animal. Life is in the blood Heb. 9:22.
Noah builds a boat Gen. 6.	Wickedness increases. Noah is righteous. He believes God and enters the boat. Flood destroys wicked. God is a judge Heb. 9:27.
Confusion of tongues Gen. 11.	Man tried to reach God. He confuse their languages and each tribe scat tered his own way Rom. 3:23,10-12; Isa. 53:6.
Abraham offers Isaac Gen. 22.	God provides a ram to take Isaac's place. Man should die for he is a sinner. The animal sacrifice lets man live Mark 10:45.

Moses overcomes Pharaoh Ex. 6:6,7; 7:11.	God gives Moses great power Gen. 18:14. Rivers turn to blood. Frogs like an army come out of river; gnats
From these 9 plagues choose the ones most important to your people. Show God's power over nature and creation. Compare their gods to this.	lice, swarms of flies are everywhere. The cattle are diseased. There are boils on everyone's body; great hail stones destroyed the crops. Locusts are at everything on the farms and heavy darkness is over the land.
The Passover in Egypt Ex. 12.	The firstborn is killed unless blood is on the doorpost Exod. 12:13.
God's Ten Laws Ex. 19,20.	Love God with all your heart - love your neighbor as yourself Matt. 22: 37-39. Have you kept *all* of God's laws? James 2:10.
Elijah on Mt. Carmel 1 Kings 18.	Elijah overcomes the prophets of Baal. God is greater than any witchcraft, sorcery 18:39.
John the Baptist announces Jesus Christ Luke 3:1-22.	God is saying a Saviour is coming. Get ready for Him 3:4,6. He is saying the same to you. Get ready to accept Jesus.
Jesus Christ is born Luke 1:26-35; 4:1-13.	Jesus is greater than Satan. He makes him go away defeated. Can your god defeat Satan?
Jesus overcomes demons Mark 5:1-20	Satan and his workers all obey Jesus. What do people fear the most? Sorcery, demons, witchcraft, maita? All are subject to Jesus Christ Matt. 28:18.
Jesus raises dead girl Mark 5:35-42	Jesus can give life. He has power over death John 14:6; 11:25,27. Death is a man's greatest enemy.
Five thousand eat bread and fish Mark 6:33-44.	Jesus caused the food to satisfy everyone. He didn't want anyone to go away hungry. He is concerned about our physical needs John 6:35.
The Lord of the farm and the tenants Mark 12:1-11.	The farmers rebelled and even slew the son and it is with anyone who refuses Christ. Explain John 3:36. Jesus is the Son.

Trial and crucifixion of Jesus
Mark 14,15. (You may take several weeks here).
Talk about believing in Jesus.
Give examples of it and what it means.

Tell what happened. Explain that He died for all people. He took their places. Use Luke 23:39-43. One rejected; one believed. Isa. 53:6; 1 Pet. 2:24. Jesus is God's perfect sacrifice for sin for all time.

Resurrection of Jesus Christ
Mark 16 and Luke 24:1-11.
Further explanation on believing.

Jesus is now Lord of all. He is able to save completely those who come to God by HIM   Heb. 7:25; Romans 10:9-13.

Ascension and return
Acts 1:8-11

Tell what it is to trust Jesus.

Jesus stayed for 40 days and then returned to His Father. He will return to judge the world. He is preparing a home for His children John 14:1-3.

New life in Christ. How it happened for Cornelius
Acts 10:34-43

Emphasize that all of the people in Cornelius' house believed together. They all sang, praised God and witnessed to each other. They received new life and entered God's family. Invite them to receive Christ and follow Him.

****

Without doubt many have now believed. This is not the work of man. It is the work of the Holy Spirit. Some of these may not understand very well. But they have turned from idols to serve the living God, so help them now to a better understanding. As they hear the word and pray they will grow.

D.
Media Strategy for Target Groups

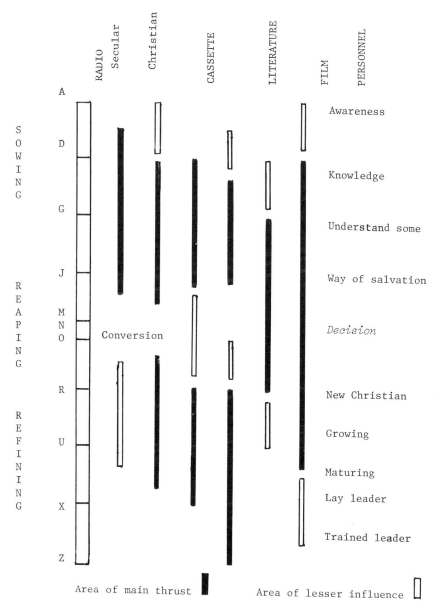

Area of main thrust ▮   Area of lesser influence ▯

E.

Maps

NIGERIA FEB 1976

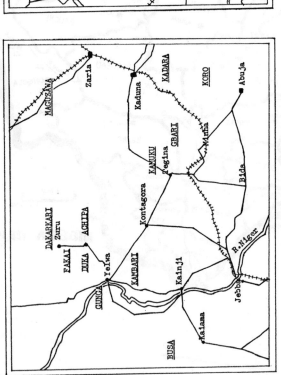

NORTH WEST

approx. 50 miles

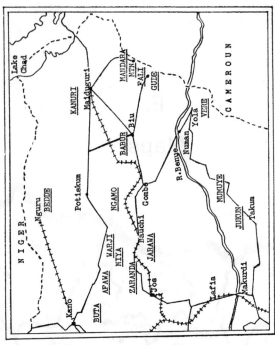

NORTH EAST

approx. 100 miles

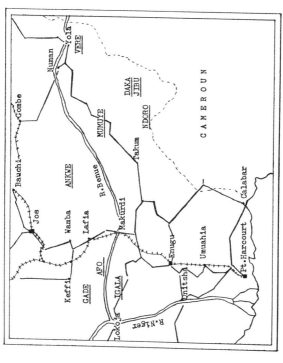

BENUE VALLEY

approx.100 miles

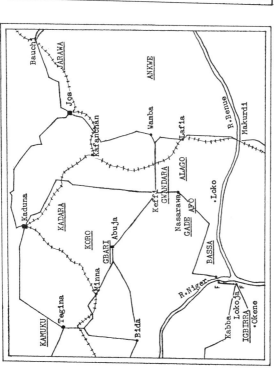

CENTRAL

approx.50 miles

F.

Epilogue

Resumé of Report on Consultation Frontier Situations in Central Nigeria, March 17,18, 1976, Jos, Nigeria

The consultation was convened by the General Secretary of the Nigeria Evangelical Fellowship for the purpose of:

1. Providing an understanding of scope and rationale of research
2. Presenting the implications for future gospel ministry
3. Taking the first step in implementation

Suggested steps to be taken were:

1. Pass this information to every level of church organization with intent to enlist every member in the task
2. Translation of the text into Hausa and possibly Yoruba
3. Denominations conduct strategy planning sessions at district levels; and at regional levels interdenominational planning
4. Undertake recruitment and training of workers as soon as possible with special attention on cultural training
5. New emphasis in all Bible Training institutions on Church Planting
6. Church missionary organizations need to be alerted and enlisted

7. Supporting departments such as Community/Rural Development, Medical, Literature, Radio need to be informed and integrated into the task
8. Appropriate tools need to be developed:
    a) Enlargement of Lesson Series Appendix C
    b) New Life for All books for understanding of the gospel and followup
    c) Tracts for literates and illiterates
    d) Cassette tapes in various languages
    e) Discipling literature such as Steps to Baptism

In conclusion, all of us were acutely aware of the awesome size of the task before us as we considered that it involves 2 - 2½ millions of people most of whom are illiterate, isolated from the main stream of Nigerian life and still holding to many traditional forms of religion. But we were also very conscious of the fact that some of them are discarding the old ways for newer ones. Changes are taking place. God is already at work. Hence there was an unmistakable urgency in our discussions. This task will require nothing less than the total mobilization of the churches of Nigeria if we are to evangelize these people by 1980. The Holy Spirit working through us is able to do this.

Bibliography

ALLEN, Roland
   The Spontaneous Expansion of the Church.   Grand Rapids:
      Eerdmans Publishing Co. 1962.
   Missionary Methods: St. Paul's and Ours?   Grand Rapids:
      Eerdmans Publishing Co., 1962

BEAVER, R. Pierce, Editor.   The Gospel and Frontier Peoples.
   Pasadena: William Carey Library, 1973.

BELLAMY, Wilfred A., Editor.   West African Congress on Evangelism.
   Jos, Nigeria: Nigeria Evangelical Fellowship and New Life
      for All, 1968.

COVELL, Ralph R., WAGNER, C. Peter. An Extension Seminary Primer.
   Pasadena: William Carey Library, 1971.

DOUGLAS, J.D., Editor.   Let the Earth Hear His Voice.   Minneapolis:
   World Wide Publications, 1975.

FORDE, Daryll, Editor.   Ethnography Survey of Africa.   London:
   International African Institute, 1956

   GUNN, Harold D.   Pagan Peoples of Central Area Northern
      Nigeria. 1956 Part 12.

GUNN, and CONANT. Peoples of Plateau Area. 1953. Part 7.
    Peoples of Niger-Benue Confluence. Part 10.
    Peoples of Mid Nigeria. Part 15. 1960.

Bassa	Pt. 12	pp. 71–85
Jimbim Miya Sirawa	Pt. 12	pp. 11–16
Warji	Pt. 12	pp. 22–33
Butawa	Pt. 12	pp. 76–78
Dakarkari	Pt. 15	pp. 29–49
(Includes Fakawa Bangawa Lilawa)		
Gbari	Pt. 15	pp. 85–109
Koro	Pt. 15	pp. 109–127
Gwandara	Pt. 15	pp. 118–120
Jarawa	Pt. 7	pp. 60–74
Kadara	Pt. 15	pp. 122–137
Kambari	Pt. 15	pp. 21–29
Gungawa	Pt. 15	pp. 11–20

GRIMLEY, John B., & ROBINSON, Gordon E. Church Growth in Central
    and Southern Nigeria. Grand Rapids: Eerdmans Publishing Co.
    1966.

HILL, D. Leslie. Designing a Theological Ecucation by Extension
    Program. Pasadena: William Carey Library, 1974.

LIAO, David C.E. The Unresponsive, Resistant or Neglected?
    Chicago: Moody Press, 1970.

McGAVRAN, Donald. Understanding Church Growth. Grand Rapids:
    Eerdmans, 1970.
    How Churches Grow. New York: Friendship Press, 1955.

MEEK, C.K. The Northern Tribes of Nigeria. London: Oxford
    University Press, 1925. Two volumes.

Gudi – Fali	Vol. 1	pp. 293–312	
Mumuye	Vol. 1	pp. 436–531	
Vere	Vol. 1	pp. 413–445	
Ngamo	Vol. 2	pp. 269–289	
Jibu	Vol. 2	pp. 499–519	
Sukur	Vol. 1	pp. 312–320	
Daka	Vol. 1	pp. 328–342	Ethno on Chamba

    Tribal Studies. 1931 London: K. Paul Trench & Trubner,
    1971 reprint.

MURDOCK, G.P. Africa - Its Peoples and Culture History. New
    York: McGraw Hill, 1959.

    African Cultural Summaries. New Haven H.R.A.F. (Human Re-
    lations Area Files) available in some universities and
    colleges.

PENTECOST, Edward C. Reaching the Unreached. Pasadena: William Carey Library, 1974.

PICKETT, J.W., WARNSHUIS, A.L., SINGH, C.H., McGAVRAN, D.A. Church Growth and Group Conversion. Pasadena: William Carey Library, 5th edition 1973.

SMALLEY, William A. Readings in Missionary Anthropology. Pasadena: William Carey Library, 1974.

SOGAARD, Viggo B. Cassette Ministry. Minneapolis: Bethany Fellowship, Inc. 1975

TEMPLE, O. Notes on Tribes, Provinces, Emirates and Northern States of Nigeria. Compiled from official reports. Lagos: C.M.S. Bookshop, 1922. Reprint London: Frank Cass & Co., 1965. Following are tribes and pages:

Afo (Afu)	Page	1	Gbari	Page 120
Afawa	Page	3	Igbirra	Page 154
Ankwe	Page	18	Jarawa	Page 165
Alago	Page	26	Kadara	Page 172
Bassa	Page	41	Kambari	Page 198
Busa	Page	74	Kamuku	Page 205
Buta	Page	76	Koro	Page 238
Dakarkari	Page	88	Maguzawa	Page 263
Gade	Page	108	Mumuye	Page 287
Ngamo	Page	110	Vere	Page 357
Gwandara	Page	118	Warji	Page 362

WAGNER, C. Peter. Frontiers in Missionary Strategy. Chicago: Moody Press, 1970.

JOURNALS AND PAPERS

CONANT, F.P. *JARAWA*. Africa Vol. 33 (3). 1963:227-236.

FAFF, Bernard. A Fertility Figure of Unrecorded Style from Northern Nigeria. *AFU*. Man XLVIII. p. 125.

FITZPATRICK, Jos. F.J. *KAMUKU* in Journal African Society Vol. 11 (43) April 1912:332-338. Customs.

HAFFENDEN, Wilson. *IGBIRRA*. In Journal African Society, Vol. 29 (116) 1930:370-375.

JACOBS, Donald R. The Homogeneity and Diversity of African Cultures as a Background to Educational Cooperation. Lecture presented at A.E.A.M. Christian Education Strategy Conference, Nairobi, January 1973.

KATO, Byang H. Evangelization and Culture. An address given
    at the National Congress on Evangelization Ife University
    August 23, 1975.

MACFIE, J.W. Scott, *BASSA BURIAL* in Man. Vol. 11, Art. 103, 1911
    pp. 185,186.

NA'IBI, Shaibu. *GADE* in Nigeria Magazine Vol. 59, 1958:288-307.
    GBARI in Nigeria Magazine special publication 1960.
    GBARI, KORO in Chronicle of Abuja, 1962:83-87.

NEHER, G. *SUKUR* in Nigeria Field, Jan. 1964:16-27. Brass Casing.

NICHOLSON, J. *BUSA, BORGU* in Journal African Society, Vol. 26
    #102, pp. 92-100, January 1927.

SETON, R.S. Installation of an Attah of Idah. J.R.A.I. LVIII
    pp. 255-278
    Notes on Igala Tribe. J.R.A.I. XXIX. pp. 42-52.

The author, Gerald (Jerry) Swank, has lived and worked in Nigeria with the Sudan Interior Mission since 1940. After a term of pioneer evangelism he reorganized the Kagoro Bible Training School in central Nigeria and directed it for 17 years. He developed several innovative concepts of leadership training which continue to produce fruitful results and to serve as models for similar training institutions.

In 1963 he founded the movement of New Life for All and directed it for five years. This became a dynamic program of evangelism aimed at mobilizing the Church in Nigeria for the purpose of thoroughly saturating every community with the gospel of our Lord Jesus Christ. New Life for All has since spread into a score of other African nations. Subsequently he became the first Secretary for Evangelism and Church Growth for the Evangelical Churches of West Africa (SIM related).

Throughout these years he has demonstrated a deep and abiding commitment to the task of evangelism and church planting, and particularly that every ethnic group and every person may have an adequate understanding of Jesus Christ and the opportunity to accept Him. Certainly God has prepared His servant to write this book.

BOOKS BY THE WILLIAM CAREY LIBRARY

GENERAL

The Birth of Missions in America by Charles L. Chaney, $7.95 paper, 352 pp.

Education of Missionaries' Children: The Neglected Dimension of World Mission by D. Bruce Lockerbie, $1.95 paper, 76 pp.

The Holdeman People: The Church in Christ, Mennonite, 1859-1969 by Clarence Hiebert, $7.95 cloth, 688 pp.

On the Move with the Master: A Daily Devotional Guide on World Mission by Duain W. Vierow, $4.95 paper, 176 pp.

Tips on Taping: Language Recording in the Social Sciences by Wayne and Lonna Dickerson, $4.95x paper, 208 pp.

STRATEGY OF MISSION

Church Growth and Christian Mission by Donald A. McGavran, $4.95x paper, 256 pp.

Church Growth and Group Conversion by Donald A. McGavran et al., $2.45 paper, 128 pp.

Committed Communities: Fresh Streams for World Missions by Charles J. Mellis, $3.95 paper, 160 pp.

The Conciliar-Evangelical Debate: The Crucial Documents, 1964-1976 edited by Donald McGavran, $8.95 paper, 400 pp.

Crucial Dimensions in World Evangelization edited by Arthur F. Glasser et al., $6.95x paper, 480 pp.

Evangelical Missions Tomorrow edited by Wade T. Coggins and Edwin L. Frizen, Jr., $5.95 paper, 208 pp.

Everything You Need to Grow a Messianic Synagogue by Phillip E. Goble, $2.45 paper, 176 pp.

Growth and Life in the Local Church by H. Boone Porter, $2.95 paper, 124 pp.

Here's How: Health Education by Extension by Ronald and Edith Seaton, $3.45 paper, 144 pp.

A Manual for Church Growth Surveys by Ebbie C. Smith, $3.95 paper, 144 pp.

Reaching the Unreached by Edward C. Pentecost, $5.95 paper, 245 pp.

Readings in Third World Missions: A Collection of Essential Documents edited by Marlin L. Nelson, $6.95x paper, 304 pp.

AREA AND CASE STUDIES

Aspects of Pacific Ethnohistory by Alan R. Tippett, $3.95 paper, 216 pp.

The Baha'i Faith: Its History and Teachings by William M. Miller, $8.95 paper, 450 pp.

A Century of Growth: The Kachin Baptist Church of Burma by Herman Tegenfeldt, $9.95 cloth, 540 pp.

Christ Confronts India by B.V. Subbamma, $4.95 paper, 238 pp.

Church Growth in Burundi by Donald Hohensee, $4.95 paper, 160 pp.

Church Growth in Japan by Tetsunao Yamamori, $4.95 paper, 184 pp.

Church Planting in Uganda: A Comparative Study by Gailyn Van Rheenen, $4.95 paper, 192 pp.

Circle of Harmony: A Case Study in Popular Japanese Buddhism by Kenneth J. Dale, $4.95 paper, 238 pp.

Crucial Issues in Bangladesh by Peter McNee, $6.95 paper, 304 pp.

The Emergence of a Mexican Church by James E. Mitchell, $2.95 paper, 184 pp.

The Growth Crisis in the American Church: A Presbyterian Case Study by Foster H. Shannon, $4.95 paper, 176 pp.

The How and Why of Third World Missions: An Asian Case Study by Marlin L. Nelson, $6.95 paper, 256 pp.

La Serpiente y la Paloma (La Iglesia Apostolica de la Fe en Jesucristo de Mexico) by Manual J. Gaxiola, $2.95 paper, 194 pp.

People Movements in the Punjab by Margaret and Frederick Stock, $8.95 paper, 388 pp.

Profile for Victory: New Proposals for Missions in Zambia by Max Ward Randall, $3.95 cloth, 224 pp.

The Protestant Movement in Bolivia by C. Peter Wagner, $3.95 paper, 264 pp.

The Protestant Movement in Italy: Its Progress, Problems, and Prospects by Roger E. Hedlund, $3.95 paper, 266 pp.

Protestants in Modern Spain: The Struggle for Religious Pluralism by Dale G. Vought, $3.45 paper, 168 pp.

The Religious Dimension in Hispanic Los Angeles by Clifton L. Holland, $9.95 paper, 550 pp.

The Role of the Faith Mission: A Brazilian Case Study by Fred Edwards, $3.45 paper, 176 pp.

Solomon Islands Christianity: A Study in Growth and Obstruction by Alan R. Tippett, $5.95x paper, 432 pp.

Taiwan: Mainline Versus Independent Church Growth by Allen J. Swanson, $3.95 paper, 300 pp.

Tonga Christianity by Stanford Shewmaker, $3.45 paper, 164 pp.

Treasure Island: Church Growth Among Taiwan's Urban Minnan Chinese by Robert J. Bolton, $6.95 paper, 416 pp.

Understanding Latin Americans by Eugene A. Nida, $3.95 paper, 176 pp.

A Yankee Reformer in Chile: The Life and Works of David Trumbull by Irven Paul, $3.95 paper, 172 pp.

THEOLOGICAL EDUCATION BY EXTENSION

Principios del Crecimiento de la Iglesia by Wayne C. Weld and Donald A. McGavran, $3.95 paper, 448 pp.

Principles of Church Growth by Wayne C. Weld and Donald A. McGavran, $4.95x paper, 400 pp.

HIEBERT LIBRARY

3 6877 00039 7371

The World Directory of Theological Education by Extension by Wayne C. Weld, $5.95x paper, 416 pp. *1976 Supplement only,* $1.95x, 64 pp.

Writing for Theological Education by Extension by Lois McKinney, $1.45x paper, 64 pp.

APPLIED ANTHROPOLOGY

Becoming Bilingual: A Guide to Language Learning by Donald Larson and William A. Smalley, $5.95x paper, 426 pp.

Christopaganism or Indigenous Christianity? edited by Tetsunao Yamamori and Charles R. Taber, $5.95 paper, 242 pp.

The Church and Cultures: Applied Anthropology for the Religious Worker by Louis J. Luzbetak, $5.95x paper, 448 pp.

Culture and Human Values: Christian Intervention in Anthropological Perspective (writings of Jacob Loewen) edited by William A. Smalley, $5.95 paper, 466 pp.

Customs and Cultures: Anthropology for Christian Missions by Eugene A. Nida, $3.95x paper, 322 pp.

Manual of Articulatory Phonetics by William A. Smalley, $4.95x paper, 522 pp.

Message and Mission: The Communication of the Christian Faith by Eugene A. Nida, $3.95x paper, 254 pp.

Readings in Missionary Anthropology edited by William A. Smalley, $5.95x paper, 384 pp.

POPULARIZING MISSION

Defeat of the Bird God by C. Peter Wagner, $4.95 paper, 256 pp.

God's Word in Man's Language by Eugene A. Nida, $2.95 paper, 192 pp.

The Task Before Us (audiovisual) by the Navigators, $29.95, 137 slides

The 25 Unbelievable Years: 1945-1969 by Ralph D. Winter, $2.95 paper, 128 pp.

World Handbook for the World Christian by Patrick St. J. St. G. Johnstone, $4.95 paper, 224 pp.

REFERENCE

An American Directory of Schools and Colleges Offering Missionary Courses edited by Glenn Schwartz, $5.95x paper, 266 pp.

Bibliography for Cross-Cultural Workers edited by Alan R. Tippett, $4.95 paper, 256 pp.

Evangelical Missions Quarterly Vols. 7-9, $8.95x cloth, 330 pp.

The Means of World Evangelization: Missiological Education at the Fuller School of World Mission edited by Alvin Martin, $9.95 paper, 544 pp.

Protestantism in Latin America: A Bibliographical Guide edited by John H. Sinclair, $8.95x paper, 448 pp.

The World Directory of Mission-Related Educational Institutions edited by Ted Ward and Raymond Buker, Sr., $19.95x cloth, 906 pp.